IN THE SHADOW OF THE WHEEL

Heart-tugging memoirs of a coalminer's daughter

GERALDINE FARREN

FARREN BOOKS

Text Copyright © Geraldine Farren 2009

Cover design by Jo Spaul and James Fitt ©

All rights reserved. No part of this publication may be reproduced, stored in a retrieval system, or transmitted in any form or by any means, electronic, mechanical, photocopy, recording or otherwise, without prior written permission of the copyright owner. Nor can it be circulated in any form of binding or cover other than that in which it is published and without similar condition including this condition being imposed on a subsequent purchaser.

Some names in this book have been changed to protect the innocent.

ISBN 978-07552-1208-8

Authors OnLine Ltd
19 The Cinques
Gamlingay, Sandy
Bedfordshire SG19 3NU
England

This book is also available in e-book format, details of which are available at www.authorsonline.co.uk

DEDICATIONS

I dedicate this book to my dearest mother Mercia Emma. Thank you for sharing with me this wonderful story of your life.

I also dedicate this book to all the coalminers of England and Wales, past and present.

ACKNOWLEDGEMENTS

A special thank you to my daughter Tracy, for coming to the rescue every time I messed up on the computer, (which was often) even though her patience did wear thin at times.

Thanks also to my good friend Barbara, whose expertise in the field of genealogy took me the long journey back to my roots.

Thank you all my close and also extended family. Your added input of information regarding the now deceased members of the Harrison family, proved invaluable.

Thanks also to my dear friends, whose encouragement spurred me on when I started to drag my heels.

And finally, thanks all you Harrisons in the spirit world. I know you were with me every step of the way.

Frank Harrison, coal mine manager

PROLOGUE

It was on the 4th of November 1912, that I finally slid from the worn out, prolapsed womb of my mother; into the old, but capable hands of Granny Mockford, the local midwife.

Granny was certainly no stranger to these occasions. For hadn't she delivered hundreds of babies before me, in this small mining community of 'Bermuda' and the two flanking towns of 'Bedworth' and 'Nuneaton'? These places were all situated in the county of Warwickshire, England.

Granny was no stranger to my mother's birthing bed either. She'd already placed eleven more siblings into my mother's arms before I came along. Now thankfully, if only for my mother's sake, I was to be the last child to be born to my now middle-aged parents.

In the latter months of this final pregnancy, father employed a local woman from Bermuda village to help mother do her washing. This was a major task in itself, with so many children to keep clean.

It so happened that Mrs Stringer was also heavily pregnant. So the sight of the two of them, 'huffing' and 'puffing' en route to the clothes line, trying to balance baskets of freshly washed clothes onto hugely swollen bellies, must have given many local folk cause to smile.

During this time, my father was embroiled in reading a book called *The Sign of The Cross*, a fiction story based in Roman times. The hero of the book was named 'Marcus' and the heroine 'Mercia'. Thus, on the day I was born, I was duly named Mercia Emma Harrison: Emma being my mother's name too.

Father tried to persuade Mrs Stringer, who went into labour shortly afterwards, to call her newborn son Marcus. But Mrs Stringer was having none of it, and called him Alfred instead.

My father, Francis (Frank) Harrison, was the underground manager of Griff 'Clara' Colliery, which stood adjacent to Bermuda village. It was the latest shaft to have been sunk by the Newdigate Mining Company.

A short, stiff man, sturdy in stature. He sported a large, bristly, handlebar moustache, with eyebrows to match. He was a firm but fair man, held in high esteem by his men, who called him 'Gaffer' Harrison.

Father had always despised the bullying, sadistic methods used by some of his predecessors to get more work out of the men. He was much too 'earthy' for that. For hadn't he known himself what it was like to live in a family struggling to survive poverty?

He himself had been brought to his knees more than once at one time or another, by the exhaustion and fatigue a shift down the pit could bring to a man. And so did the previous generations of Harrison's before him. They'd known what poverty was like all right, poverty at its very worst.

The further back he had delved into his family's past history, he came to realise that the mining life for them, and many others, had been almost intolerable. That his own life had been comparatively easy compared with theirs. Haunted by this knowledge, Father had constantly craved a better life for us all, and he had eventually achieved it.

So now, to put this story into its full perspective, I have to go back in time for a while to give you the complete picture.

GREAT GRANDMOTHER

When my Great Grandmother Elizabeth Harrison crossed paths with local man Thomas Deeming, it was a liaison that was to cost both her and her family dearly.

Apparently, it seems Elizabeth had been a very shy, almost introverted young woman, who rarely socialised much with people outside her family or workplace. So this naive, and very unworldly girl must have felt extremely disadvantaged, when first approached by the brash, over-confident Thomas Deeming.

Obviously, at the time when these earlier dramas occurred, neither I nor my elder siblings were even born yet. But we are well armed with a wealth of snippets of family information passed down to us through the generations; these being substantiated by a strong backbone of facts provided by intensive researching within the offices of genealogy.

It only remains for me to try to speculate on how these earlier events actually unfolded. So I will now try to piece this enthralling story together.

Elizabeth Harrison walked jauntily away from the stalls of Bedworth market, swapping her heavy basket of shopping from one arm to the other. The dancing hemline of her long cotton skirt swept the dusty cobbles with each exaggerated step.

Elizabeth herself was feeling on top of the world today. The sun was shining brightly, giving a feel -good effect to everyone who basked in its energising rays. It was a great day to be out in, and she'd purchased all the vegetables and other sundries her mother had requested. Now, at last, she was ready to make her way back home.

As she walked through the town, and was passing by one of the many local pubs, Elizabeth was suddenly halted in her tracks by someone calling her name from inside its dark interior.

Never being allowed to frequent such establishments, the painfully shy girl waited with eyes downcast as a ruggedly handsome man emerged into the sunlight.

'Hello there, my beautiful,' he gushed; walking over towards her with an exaggerated air of confidence.

''Ave you got a minute for me, my darlin', cos I need a word with you?' He whispered in her ear softly, his lips brushing her hair intimately, laughing out loudly at her obvious embarrassment.

'Come on now, Lizzie,' he chuckled, 'give us yer basket; I'll walk you back 'ome.' Then, linking his arm into hers, he led the now red-faced girl up the street.

Before reaching the entrance to the yard where she lived, Thomas Deeming turned to look down on the pretty face of Elizabeth Harrison. He noted the creamy almost alabaster skin that covered the perfect apples of her high cheekbones. Also her small full lips, which were drawn slightly back, revealing even, white teeth.
Light brown hair highlighted with sun-lightened streaks, was swept up softly from her slender neck. This was loosely coiled on the top of her head, and all held together with a tortoiseshell comb.

Thomas spoke to her again: This time in a husky, impatient voice, a frown creating rippled ridges across his forehead.

'Now then, Lizzie, 'ow much longer are you gonna play this 'ard to get game with me? Cos I'm getting a bit fed up wi' it now.

I think it's about time you gave me a few straight answers; I'm not goin' to wait around forever, yer know. Cos if I'm wastin' me time with yer, just you tell me now. I know yer fancy me a bit, so don't try an' deny it.'

Elizabeth took this moment to study this older man, with his light hazel eyes, and his look: I'm a man of the world type of arrogance.

Handsome he surely was, and she knew much in demand by the local girls. She'd been both flattered and excited of late that he was showing her his attentions.

Never having walked out with a man in her life before, Elizabeth knew that this wasn't due to her looks, but to her acute shyness. It hadn't helped her ability to forge relationships with men, her father dying when she was very young. This tragedy had made her mother become over-protective of her. Men, up to now, had always taken her shyness as aloofness, and thought her unsociable. So they tended to avoid her, seeking out the more amenable ladies of the town.

Now, though, since Thomas had been showing her some interest, she had to admit she was experiencing emotions she didn't know existed. Her heart seemed to skip a beat whenever she set eyes on him. He was so good looking, he could have any girl he wanted.

She didn't want to lose him though, and was frightened he would soon get bored with her. But this was unknown territory, and she didn't know how to handle this situation. Also, his forwardness disturbed her a little, and she knew her mother wouldn't approve of him.

Sensing in her manner some hesitation, Thomas caught hold of her hand, and pulled her towards him.

'Meet me tonight up coalpit fields, Elizabeth, then we can talk wi'out bein' disturbed. We need ter sort this out once an' fer all.'

Playing on her emotions like a hooked fish, Thomas skilfully reeled her in and out.

'You must know 'ow much I wanna be with you, Lizzie. You and me, we were meant fer each other.' He continued on: his expertise at flattery again coming to the fore. 'I wouldn't be goin' to all this trouble if I didn't think you wanted me too, Lizzie. Though with the negative way you've bin respondin' to me attentions, I'm beginning ter think I've got it all wrong. Perhaps you don't really like me as much as I thought you did.

Anyway: If you come up the fields abart eight o'clock, we'll talk abart it then. If yer don't turn up, I won't bother you agen, I promise.'

And on this final note of emotional blackmail, Thomas turned and walked away, pausing only to blow her a cheeky kiss. A cocky grin spread over his face: At last he felt he was getting the upper hand in this game of chance. But how long would it take, before he could play his ace!

Elizabeth, despite all her reservations but afraid of losing him, did turn up at Coalpit fields that night, and many nights after this. The more she saw of him, the more her attraction to Thomas was becoming like a nail to a magnet, and she hung on to his every word.

An inexperienced young girl, listening gullibly to the much - practised patter of his wooing, throwing all her caution to the wind. Every time he put his arms around her waist and covered her face with his kisses, her head spun with happiness. She soon lost some of her inhibitions, returning his kisses with an equal passion. She was a willing pupil for a tutor who put her so at ease.

Thomas looked down at the smiling girl lying beside him on the grassy bank. God, she's turning out to be hard work, he thought to himself. He was fast getting bored with her now. Though he'd known she'd be a tough nut to crack, with her moralistic upbringing. Soon though, he'd have to take the bull by the horns if he was going to take her down.

Sometimes he questioned himself why he was doing this to her; a virgin. When there were so many other lusty, compliable wenches in Bedworth, whose love-making skills were compatible with his own. Elizabeth was the sort of girl you'd want to settle down with. Marriage material, I suppose you'd call it.

No way was he getting ensnared by a woman yet though. He was enjoying playing the field too much to get tied down just yet.

But then, just a few weeks ago, while having a drink down the pub, his mates had set him the ultimate challenge, and put wagers on it. To go out and conquer the 'ice maiden', they had said smugly. So now here he was, trying to keep his untarnished reputation intact. He knew he was doing wrong, because she was a nice, well brought up girl. His conscience pricked him a little, but it was only momentarily.

The happy, cheerful voice of Elizabeth broke into his thoughts.

'Tom Deeming,' she playfully chided him, her new-found confidence showing, her beautiful blue eyes now sparkling with revitalised emotion, 'will you stop starin' into space, and give me another quick cuddle. I've got to go 'ome in a minute or two or me mam will start worryin'.'

Duly obliging her, Thomas gently stroked her soft fair hair, while raining more kisses on her eager, upturned face.

Elizabeth herself was so happy: She couldn't remember another time in the whole of her life when she'd felt such overwhelming emotions. Snuggling up closely against him, she was so carried away by her own desires that she hardly noticed when his hand slipped down onto the gentle curve of her small breast.

It wasn't until he fumbled with the buttons of her dress and slid his hand furtively inside, that her survival instincts kicked in. Trying to pull away from him, Thomas held her even tighter, rocking her taut body soothingly against his own.

'Come on now, Lizzie, just relax a bit. Don't get yoursen so tensed up all the time. It's only a natural thing that we're doin', after all.

You surely should know by now that after all these weeks together we've committed oursens to each other.'

Thomas's false but tenderly spoken words gave the naive Elizabeth much needed comfort.

'You really do love me like you say yer do, don't yer, Tom?' she whispered desperately, the alarm bells still ringing in her head. 'I do need to be absolutely sure yer not just usin' me.'

Thomas replied, not really taking in anything she was saying. His voice, now thick with desire, was muffled, as he pressed his lips against her slender neck.

'Yer really must learn ter trust me a bit more, Lizzie,' he muttered.

After making this statement, Thomas lost no time in sliding his hands back inside her dress once again, his breathing now heavy with expectation.

Elizabeth didn't have time to resist: It all happened so fast. Within seconds of undoing his trouser buttons, Thomas took away all of her options. Shivering with both fright and anticipation, she felt him enter her very soul; and the pain of it all made her gasp. But afterwards, when Thomas held her to him tightly, she was reassured everything would be all right; for hadn't he said so.

Now, as he dressed himself hurriedly, Thomas spoke sharply to Elizabeth.

'You get yoursen 'ome now, Lizzie, or yer ma'll be out lookin' for yer. I 'ave to go now anyway, I've got things ter do. But I'll come and see you agen as soon as I can.'

He gave her a quick peck on her cheek, then, turning sharply on his heel, he strode away towards the town. Watching him walk away from her, Elizabeth felt bewildered, deflated, and dirty.

An icy numbness was gripping at her body. She was beginning to feel very ill at ease. She couldn't believe she'd let it happen out of wedlock. What on earth had she been thinking of? She was now, for sure, a tainted woman, she tormented herself. Thank the Lord that Thomas wanted to marry her.

NO GOING BACK

Just three weeks later, Elizabeth's normally uneventful life was now in turmoil. Firstly, it was because she hadn't seen Thomas for ages, and it was becoming despairingly obvious to her that he was avoiding her deliberately. Secondly, her monthly curse was two weeks late, and her cycle was usually very regular. This was causing a major panic within her, that defied description.

She must soon go into town, find Thomas, and talk to him. He'd stand by her if the worst came to the worst – hadn't he promised he would? She must also, she told herself, shake off these doubts about him that keep filling her head. He'd told her that he loved her, and she believed him.

She certainly loved him; her heart and body ached for him.

Saturday came round again, with still no word from Thomas. Elizabeth knew he'd be off work today, it being the weekend. More than likely he was at the pub with his mates. There was only one thing for it, she decided. She'd have to fetch him out and speak to him.

Her mother had never allowed her to go into any public houses. She thought of them as dens of iniquity. But, at this moment in time, this could be the least of her mother's worries.

Dressing herself up to her most attractive, Elizabeth chose a dress of powder blue. This dress, she knew, brought out the colour of her lovely aquamarine eyes. These, fringed by dark luxurious lashes, were her greatest asset. And she hoped Thomas would melt the moment he looked into them.

Unfortunately for Elizabeth, it wasn't to be the reunion she had hoped for. Thomas was at the pub, and willingly dropped his pint down on the bar to follow her outside. She spoke to him sharply, her desperation giving her much-needed courage.

Trying hard to fight back the tears, her voice was now shaky with pent-up emotion.

'So now then, Tom Deeming. Where 'ave you been hidin' yoursen these last three weeks, eh?' she inquired of him curtly, pulling herself together a bit. 'I wouldn't fer one minute like to think you've bin avoidin' me on purpose for some reason. You've told me often enough that you love me. But I ain't set eyes on you since you took advantage of me. Just tell me what your little game is, eh? I thought we were walkin' out together. That was what you led me to believe anyway.'

Dropping his chin down on to his chest, an embarrassed Thomas muttered guiltily through clenched teeth.

'Now you look here, Lizzie 'Arrison,' he drawled testily, 'you're getting' much too serious abart this love thing, you know. Yer a grand lookin' gel, an' you can be sure lots of blokes'll want a crack at yer. But fond as I am of you meself, I've got a lot of wild oats to sow before I settle darn wi' anyone. I certainly ain't intendin' getting' shackled to any woman just yet.'

Stung deeply by his barbed words, Elizabeth deflated like a pricked balloon. Hot tears streamed down her face, as the man of her dreams stared defiantly down on her. He avoided looking into her eyes, which were now red and puffy.

'You lied to me,' she spluttered between sobs, her shoulders shaking with the anguish she felt. 'Everythin' that you said ter me was just one big lie. You said you'd always take care of me, an' now I think I'm havin' your babby.'

On this latest hard-hitting statement from Elizabeth, Thomas's face visibly whitened.

'Bloody hell, yer can't be,' he snapped in a horrified tone; 'it were your first time. Gels don't get babbies the first time they do it; none of the others ever 'ave. So it seems to me that yer must 'ave bin 'avin it off wi' someone else.

It certainly ain't mine, so don't think fer one minute that I'm takin' the rap for it either.'

And in complete denial, he turned and walked back into the pub.

RETRIBUTION

Elizabeth, with great effort, dragged her listless, emotionally drained body back home. Now she had to face her mother, a thought that filled her with dread. How could I have let her down so badly, she thought? What a way to repay a woman who's sacrificed all ways to bring up a child on her own since the death of her husband. She felt as bad about this as being rejected by Thomas.

Breezily, Sarah opened the door to her daughter's faint knock. She was so glad of late that Elizabeth was getting out and about a bit more. She'd always blamed herself for Lizzie being so shy and introvert. She knew she'd been over-protective of the girl since her father had died. But she'd only been doing what she thought was right. Now, though, on seeing Elizabeth's tear-stained face, Sarah's heart skipped a beat.

'What on earth's the matter wi' you, our Lizzie?' she gasped. 'What's 'appened gel to get yer inta this sort a state?'

Helping the distraught girl into the house, an apprehensive Sarah pushed Elizabeth into the nearest chair, then sat down quickly beside her.

'Come on now, out wi' it, our Lizzie, what's goin' on? Are yer feelin' ill, or has someone hurt yer? Tell me.'

Elizabeth then told her anxious mother everything that had happened to her in the previous months. From the moment she'd first set eyes on Thomas Deeming, up to the events of the present day.

Sarah was beside herself...the wretchedness showing itself on her already lined face. The exaggerated drooping of the corners of her mouth reflected the despair and sickness she was feeling inside.

'Aw no, our Lizzie,' she gasped, 'I just can't believe it. I'm mortified. Of all the women here on this earth, I thought you would have been the last gel to let a man take yer darn before you were wed. Surely you must 'ave realised that Thomas Deeming would only 'ave bin after one thing, wi' his track record.

And as fer him sayin' yer can't get pregnant the first time. All I can say ter that statement is he's bloody stupider than I thought, and his luck's just run art. If you'd only told me you were seeing the likes of him, I'd 'ave stopped it.'

Barely able to speak properly, Elizabeth answered her mother's probing questions one by one.

'Oh, our mam, I really do love him, and I trusted 'im so much. It weren't for me just a casual fling. I knew at the time what we was doin' were wrong. But it all 'appened so quickly, and he said he really loved me too. I was such a fool to believe 'im, and now he's probably left me wi' a belly full of problems.

If I am 'avin a babby, how are you and me gonna manage? We can 'ardly cope now, and I'd 'ave to give up me job at the factory. And what will folks have ter say abart me? They'll all be pointing fingers at me and lookin' darn their noses.'

Sarah softened. Putting her arms around the drooping shoulders of her sobbing daughter, she gently pulled the shaking girl close.

'Look, Lizzie, we'll cope wi' it all. Whatever 'appens next, we'll both stick together on this one. But if that no good bloody Deemin' thinks he's got away wi' this episode, he can think a-bloody-gen.'

Sarah herself must have been a tormented soul, but had loyally kept her thoughts to herself until she was alone. Why hadn't she been more vigilant, and questioned Elizabeth more about her new social life? Why had she let herself assume it was the other girls at the factory Lizzie was going out with? And how come the local nosy parkers had missed this opportunity to gather the juiciest bit of gossip this year?

How she wished now that they'd come knocking on her door, spitefully sucking up to her, before dropping the bombshell that her more than perfect daughter was playing around with the one and only Thomas Deeming. If only she had known, she could have nipped it in the bud long before.

How on earth was she going to hold her head up in public ever again, she wondered. She: the person who had continuously preached to the locals on the virtues of her daughter. She: who had often let her contempt of the local trollops, as she called them, be known to all and sundry.

Now, though, the tables would be turned, and all the sniggering gossips will be shouting their poisonous remarks in her direction

Elizabeth was not a tart though; she was just the opposite. A shy, naïve girl, who until now knew nothing about the raw side of life.

And who's fault was that? Sarah already knew what the answer was to that question. If only she'd spoken more intimately to Lizzie. Talked to her about the physical side of loving a man, and how to avoid the pitfalls. Instead of trying to keep her untainted and away from the earthiness of real life.

Yes, she herself carried a lot of the blame for the situation they were in. Now they would both have to hold their heads high, and try to ignore the battery of snide taunts that would follow them through the streets. Until the novelty of their situation became old gossip, anyway.

Sarah was filled with dread, just thinking of what the future could bring them. With Lizzie's wages eventually drying up, they could be plunged into extreme poverty. There was no man's wage coming into this house to keep the wolves from the door. Still, she must keep her fears to herself, and not be negative at this point. Her gel would need all the love and support she could give. Hopefully, they'd get by, with the help of him above.

So that's how it was: Sarah staunchly supporting Elizabeth through her now confirmed confinement. Boosting her morale by telling her tales of how this new baby could enrich both their lives.

She also lost no time in informing as many of the locals as possible. Telling them of how that 'rotten sod' Thomas Deeming had duped her innocent gel, taken her down, then done a runner. Ignoring the amused looks and nudges that constantly passed between them.

A NEW LIFE

In due course, Elizabeth gave birth to a son: my grandfather. The new baby was named William Harrison, after his own maternal grandfather. Elizabeth's disgrace was written for eternity on her son's baptism certificate. It read:

'William Harrison: Bastard son of Elizabeth Harrison.'

Although they'd both tried hard to manage, it was becoming an extremely uphill struggle. With Elizabeth's job being given to someone else during her confinement, things were now getting desperate.Sarah was still taking in washing every day, but it only paid a pittance compared with Elizabeth's lost wages; just enough to cover the rent. Now, with an extra mouth to feed, the future looked bleak for them, the workhouse looming ever closer.

Thoughts of the workhouse once again sent shudders through Sarah's body. These establishments hadn't been open very long at this time. But already horror stories about them were emerging around the towns. Terrible tales of what went on behind those huge black doors.

Sarah lay in bed trying hard to recall all she'd been told. Those who were in the know had said the inmates were starving, because the little food they got was rank. Thin watery soup made from corn or rice, thickened with potato. Stale bread, and milk to drink that was sometimes so sour it was blue. They did say though that at Christmas and Easter the soup had a bit of pauper's meat boiled in it as a special treat... thanks to someone's kind charity.

People eligible for the workhouse had to be either aged, blind, infirm, have bodily defects, be mentally unstable, or destitute children. Or, like herself and Elizabeth, just unable to support themselves properly.

Paupers, when registered in, had to be bathed and their clothes fumigated. Just the thought of this indignity made Sarah feel quite faint.

Also, what would become of baby William? He for a start would be taken away from Lizzie once he'd finished nursing. Males and females were always separated from each other in the workhouse; sometimes never seeing each other ever again.

As sure as God made little apples, this would break the gel's heart, it would. They'd have to work as well, with no pay, just for their keep. But that was not a problem for them, they were both used to hard graft.

The men that were able, they said, had to break stones or grind corn, and maintain the workhouse lands and gardens. Sometimes the most able-bodied were hired out to local farmers at a cheap rate.

While the women inmates washed clothes and did mending brought in from outside. They also had to attend to the resident kids, the old, and the sick. Even these kids were made to do work when barely old enough. Things apparently got much worse too, if any of the inmates broke the rules of the house. Not that she could see herself or Elizabeth doing anything like that. Using insulting behaviour such as bad language, or not washing themselves properly - inmates were thrashed for that.

Neglecting work or pretending sickness, even entering other wards looking for their loved ones. This could mean confinement, sometimes without food and water for days. Striking an inmate or member of staff, when you couldn't take any more, meant a referral to the magistrate. And God only knows what happened to the poor devils then.

All these terrible visions whirled around and around inside Sarah's throbbing head. Thomas Neale, who'd done odd building jobs in the workhouse at times, now refused to go any more. He said the inmates slept on the floor on slightly raised boards. Lying on straw-filled sacks that were crawling with lice.These lice and the damp conditions, he said, were responsible for multiple deaths from dysentery and pneumonia. The lice spreading typhus from person to person.
Sarah shuddered again at the thought of crawling lice. How could they both survive in such conditions, when they'd always kept themselves so clean.

Mrs Bates, just down the road, was a nurse in the Bedworth workhouse. She'd told the locals that there were so many deaths, they used what they called a sliding coffin. This, after you'd tipped the body out into the grave, could be used over and over again. She'd also said, treatment for the lunatics in there was non-existent. That they were looked after by other inmates or inexperienced nurses.

Some of them had to be tied in their beds all day. And as there was no sound-proofing, the other inmates had to try and sleep at night through the constant screaming and wailing. God help any poor bugger that has to go in that place, she had said.

Her fear of going into the workhouse had made Sarah sick to her stomach. The only glimmer of hope she could cling to was that perhaps over time rumours had been exaggerated. That it wasn't as bad as people made out. She hugged herself comfortingly and hoped this was so. After all, everyone likes to add a bit more to a juicy bit of gossip, didn't she herself know it.

Why then was she thinking so negatively all the time, she asked herself. Surely there had to be some light at the end of the tunnel. Though the thought of what could become of them still didn't bear thinking about, Sarah knew that she had to think more positively.

What was the alternative for them both then, she mulled; starvation, perhaps. Surely that would be better than dying of some disease. Her head ached even more, trying to find a solution. But she daren't tell Elizabeth of her fears.

DIVINE INTERVENTION

Sarah's hatred for Thomas Deeming consumed her so much sometimes, it frightened her. Everything they had ever had, and had struggled to hold on to after her husband's death, was now being taken away from them.

Taken away by that man's despicable moment of pleasure in deflowering an innocent, if somewhat stupid, young girl Thinking of what might be coming to them in the near future left her sleepless and sweating in her bed at night.

Surely there has to be another alternative for us, she thought to herself. I'm probably jumping the gun worrying about the workhouse at this stage; it's not as if we're destitute yet. I must ask more questions around the right people. Someone, somewhere, must have the information we need, and can throw us a lifeline.

And she was right: There are other possibilities open to you, she was told by those in the know. And these options were explained to her in great depth.

Discussing all she'd been told with her daughter that night, an excited Sarah was quick to show Elizabeth there was a way out for them.

'I've bin askin' around everywhere, Lizzie, and it seems that all's not lost; we can get some 'elp. Apparently, the parish council won't stand the cost of admittin' people inta the workhouse if they can avoid it.

And bein' as the babby's father is still in the parish, and not done a runner, they've told me what we can do. You're ter get yoursen darn ter the parish overseer's office, as soon as possible, an' let them serve what they call a bastardy bond on that no good Deemin'.If anyone on this earth needs to get 'is come-uppence, it's that one.

Why should we starve, while that bugger struts around like nothin's 'appened?'

Later that night, alone in the privacy of her bedroom, Sarah let go of all the pent-up emotions she had bottled up over the last few months. Kneeling by her bed, she whispered through the sobs that racked her weary body.
'Thank yer so much, Lord; we'll be forever in your debt.'

The justices did in fact play their part:
On the evidence of Elizabeth, Thomas was soon served with his bond (of which I have obtained a copy from the records office), and it reads as follows:

That: On the tenth day of January 1829, Elizabeth Harrison did give birth to a male bastard child, in the house of her mother Sarah Harrison. And that the said bastard child is now chargeable to the parish.

And that furthermore: Thomas Deeming of Bedworth did beget the said bastard child, on the body of Elizabeth Harrison.

Therefore: We now do order, that the said Thomas Deeming, will pay the overseer's the sum of sixteen shillings, for and towards maintenance of the said child. Also payment of fourteen shillings expenses incidental to the birth.

And furthermore, we order that Thomas Deeming, shall pay the overseer's the weekly sum of two shillings. This for as long as the said bastard child is chargeable to the parish.

And that Elizabeth Harrison shall also pay one shilling weekly.

Sarah and Elizabeth must have been ecstatic: I can imagine them leaping about the court room, hugging each other tightly, laughing and crying at the same time. Justice had been done; it was like a huge weight had been lifted from their shoulders; now they could get on with their lives.

But the result would not have pleased everyone.

Thomas, sitting scowling in the side row, would have been far from delighted with the verdict.

For him it would mean big changes. Less money in his hands to play with, meant he would have to curb his wild ways a bit, and I bet the thought of that didn't bide too well at that moment.

ALL AT A PRICE

The effect that all this had on my great-grandfather's pocket can only be shown in the fact that within weeks of being served the bond, Thomas started to woo Elizabeth again, promising his fidelity, and that he'd always be a good father to his offspring. Probably finding it cheaper to marry her, than to pay up to the parish.

Within six months of receiving the bond, Thomas took a radiant Elizabeth to the church altar. Having regained her former figure, she looked beautiful in the pale green dress her mother had made for her.

The little pink rosebuds edging the bodice, matching the real ones she wore in her hair.

Thomas also looked very smart: Wearing his brown, slightly faded, hand-me-down suit, with a crisp, freshly starched shirt, and a tie. Together with the shoes he'd borrowed from his brother, bright and shiny on his feet, he looked even more handsome than ever.

Far from feeling he'd been trapped into this wedding, Thomas was now happy about things. Elizabeth was a good-looking gel, and hadn't his mother said time enough he should settle darn with a decent woman. And to top it all, Lizzie had given him what all men want, a son. He'd do the right thing by the lad now, he would.

Unfortunately though, the marriage came too late to give baby William his rightful surname. And that's how it came about that grandfather remained a Harrison, while all the following siblings of the marriage were named Deeming.

Thomas and Elizabeth started off their married life in Leicester Street, Bedworth.

Elizabeth gave birth to several more babies, most of which died at varying ages; her second son, Henry, being the only one besides William to survive. But, despite these setbacks, they were truly happy together. Elizabeth was still as much in love with Thomas as she'd always been, and Thomas was contented too.

Sadly though, Elizabeth herself was not deemed to live a long life. Blissfully happy in her marriage to Thomas, even the loss of her beloved babies had been overcome, with him there to share her grief. Lately though, things had changed. She didn't feel so well, and she knew she was losing weight. Sometimes she found the day-to-day running of the house and the boisterous antics of the boys hard to cope with; she felt so sick and lethargic. Then other days she would rally herself back, ignoring the crippling symptoms which came to persecute her time and time again.

Thomas had started to notice the difference in her too. The death-like pallor of her skin, and her lack of appetite. But when he questioned her about it, she fobbed him off, feigning she had a feverish cold. She must be strong for her boys and Thomas, she told herself as the weeks went by. They'd all been through much too much together, to throw it all away now.

Unfortunately, though, Time didn't throw Elizabeth a lifeline. The persistent cough she'd experienced over the last few months was now getting much worse. It racked through her body day and night, leaving her chest feeling raw and painful inside. The sputum she coughed into her hanky was now tinged pink; sometimes it was even red. The complaint itself left her feeling tired, sickly, and wretched.

Elizabeth enlisted the help of her mother, Sarah, to help her cope with the heavier jobs, always making sure Thomas was at work when she came.

'If he thinks I'm coping with my chores, he won't worry so much,' she told her anxious mother. 'Hopefully, in a little while, this dratted malady will go away from me.'

Sarah wasn't so optimistic though: she had seen these symptoms too many times before, and knew her daughter would have a fight on her hands to overcome this latest challenge that was blighting her happiness once again.

Gradually, as the weeks went by, Elizabeth was slowly brought to her knees, as the illness razed the life from her body.

Eventually diagnosed as consumption (now known as tuberculosis), Elizabeth's illness took her to the grave at the age of thirty-five, leaving her boys and a devastated Thomas behind her.

LIFE MUST GO ON

Thomas now wanted to make a fresh start after Elizabeth's death. The little cottage held too many sad memories for both him and the children. Apart from that, his wages were barely enough to cover his rent. What with two growing boys, and having to pay someone to look after them while he did his stint at the mine, money was tight. Granted, his mother-in-law was good these days, having the children whenever she could. Considering how he'd ruffled her feathers when he'd rejected Elizabeth, Sarah had become exceptionally supportive once he'd towed the line.

Thomas didn't stay too long on his own though. A man had his needs, and the boys badly missed having their mother. He eventually met, and started courting, a Coventry girl named Ann. A good homely girl, quite pretty, but lacking Elizabeth's elegance. Still, she was more than capable of taking care of his sons William and Henry, and perhaps even producing a few more.

Once married again, Thomas moved them all into his widowed mother's little terraced house on The Roadway, Bedworth. It wasn't the poshest of places, but at least it was always clean. He felt he fitted in here, living alongside other residents who were struggling to make ends meet on meagre pit wages. And now, thanks to Ann, they were all happy again.

As my grandfather William used to say, 'It were nothing unusual to 'ave six kids in a bed, three one end, and three t'uther. And the women scrubbed their doorsteps every day, come rain or shine. Stopping only fer a good gab wi' anyone who passed by 'em. We were all in the same boat. Worked ter death, got no money, but allas sociable. Ready to help each other art if it were needed.'

Time passed by quickly, with Ann and Thomas producing another brood of their own. Stepbrothers and stepsisters, all welcomed by William and Henry. Thomas, for all his past faults, worked hard and long down on the face at the Charity mine.

It was no easy job to do, not when your back was breaking, and your knees were raw. Chipping coal from the ceilings of tunnels that were hardly high enough to stand up in. Your hands constantly calloused and split, from handling the sharp lumps of coal.

This wasn't helped either by the greedy mine owners, always demanding more and more from a man. Working them for long stretches at a time, sometimes in near total darkness. The candle in its holder fixed to his helmet, barely producing a glimmer of light to work by.

Often they had to make holes in the floor with their picks to accommodate their knees; when the ceilings became so low they were unable to stand at all. Their half-naked bodies were constantly coated with thick black coal dust. This attached itself to the glistening sweat that dripped from every pore. The dust, finding its way into eyes and lungs, often brought with it a death sentence.

Working waist high in water was a common enough occurrence too. And you couldn't count on being there the next day either, as roof falls were common and the death toll high. When this happened, often an under-aged son would replace his father down the mine, to keep his mother and siblings from the workhouse door. Diseases were rife here too: these swept in and out of the communities, fuelled by the lack of sanitation that extreme poverty brought with it.

Diseases like scarlet fever, smallpox, and the consumption that had taken Elizabeth.

All these could wipe out entire families, the young and the old being the most vulnerable. The local graveyards were already filling up, due to past epidemics.

Thomas drove himself on, although sometimes it was to the limit of his endurance, rather than let his children go hungry. At least, though, he had the comfort of knowing they were all happy. His children, they expected nothing, and they got nothing, but they had got each other, and the house was filled with playful laughter most of the time.

For, God forbid, it would be soon enough that his lads would have to come down to reality. William, for a start, would soon be eleven and ready to follow him down the mine.

WILLIAM THE BOY

Grandfather William didn't have the best of starts in life. Apart from the knowledge that, on his father's early rejection of him, he'd been christened Harrison instead of Deeming which had always made him feel slightly alienated from his siblings, William carried the extra burden of being quite, but not totally, deaf. On the plus side though, he was a big, strong, healthy lad, who had inherited his father's rugged good looks.

His first job when he started at the 'Winnings Pit', Hawkesbury, Coventry, was to throw the cut coal into empty wagons. When these wagons were full, they were soon towed away by sturdy little pit ponies. These strong little animals pulled the heavy wagons up the sloping tunnels to the surface, ready for the coal to be loaded onto the waiting trains; the empty wagons then being sent back down again to be refilled.

For William and the other younger workmates, it all seemed never-ending. No sooner had they filled one tub up, another empty one was there in its place. This hardly gave them enough time to straighten their aching backs. And if they did straighten up, they were shouted at by the overseer to get a move on or be sacked.

This work brought each of them, every day, to the very brink of exhaustion. After each shift, William could hardly drag himself home, he was so tired. Every step he took required so much effort.

Stepmother Ann would already have the tin bath filled with warm water on the hearth by the fire, when he walked in. The look on her face was always full of concern for him.

'God, you look knackered agen tonight, lad,' she said sympathetically, her heart going out to him. She spoke again softly, as she carefully lifted the coat from his sore shoulders.

'Get yoursen inta the bath and relax a bit, William, while I get you a cuppa tea.'

Leaving his clothes on the floor where they fell, William took no prompting.

Sliding himself into the warm, inviting water, it quickly started to soothe away the aches and pains that stabbed at him within his joints.

Placing his tea on the hearth, Ann reached up into the cupboard above to retrieve a small jar of green ointment. Kneeling down beside him, her eyes took in the many cuts and abrasions festering all over his body, where sharp shards of coal had sliced through his soft young skin. How she wished a miracle would happen to spare the boys from this dreadful way of life. If their father found the going tough, what must this young one, only a lad, be going through?

William winced sharply as she applied the pungent ointment, so she teased him affably.

'You'll soon 'ave more scars on yer body, m'lad, than that old fightin' cock in the yard,' she jested. 'N'ere mind, you'll soon toughen up when you get used ter the work; it's early days for you yet.'

William was very fond of his stepmother. She had always been there for him, never once showing any preferential treatment to her own children. It was only when he felt a bit down in the dumps that his thoughts went back to Elizabeth, his own birth mother.

Sometimes, as he lay in the darkness of his bedroom on these depressing days, he could swear he could smell the sweet odour of her skin, just like he used to whenever he'd nuzzled his face into her small bosom, and had felt the soft brush of her lips on his forehead, as she'd rocked him to and fro.

He didn't have these dreams so often any more though. Time healed all, and he was living in a very happy household.

Thomas and Ann watched all their family in turn grow up. It wasn't easy watching each son have to endure the mine at so tender an age. But mining was the only thing available to them, and you'd have to think yourself lucky to have a job at all.

There were plenty of poor devils in the workhouse who'd endured poverty, even starvation; just because they couldn't work for one reason or another. If these people hadn't been taken in by the parish overseer's, they'd all have died, that's for certain. Now, at least, they were getting some food in their bellies.

But even so; though the conditions in those places were fast improving, they were still abysmal. Ann consistently thanked the Lord nightly for what they'd got. Mining might be hard, wages poor, sometimes not enough food to go round. The children's clothes were patched and handed down one to the other as they grew. But at least they could all cuddle up together on a cold night, and they had their freedom.

Reflecting on her life with Thomas, Ann felt that she'd been privileged when they had met. Moved by his saddened demeanour, her motherly instincts had taken over, and she'd willingly opened her arms to him, offering comfort where it was badly needed. Thomas had rewarded her, in time, by eventually realising that a man could find love again.

He knew Elizabeth was irreplaceable, but was realising more and more that Ann was too; caring and considerate to him, and loving towards his children. Thomas was melting in the sincerity and warmth of this fine, gentle woman, and she always reciprocated his love.

Sadly, though, the mine gave, but it also took away.

Just as things were looking good for the family, especially now the boys were working bringing in extra money, Thomas was killed in a pit accident. A breaking pit prop caused a roof to fall down on the face at the Charity mine, and Thomas was buried under the falling debris.

According to the court revelations, at the following inquest (printed in the local Coventry paper):

It was stated that after desperate efforts by his work colleagues to remove the debris, some using only their bare hands to remove the rubble, Thomas Deeming was dug out alive, saying to his rescuers, 'I'm dyin', I'm dyin'.'

And die he did, leaving a distraught Ann to bring up his children alone. At the age of sixty-six years, he was considered to have had a reasonably long life. Nothing it seemed could be taken for granted in the life of a mining family.

WILLIAM THE MAN

By the time Thomas Deeming had met his unfortunate end, his eldest son, my grandfather William, had already left home. Whether it was because of his deafness, or because the girl of his dreams hadn't yet come on the scene, is unknown. But it had been quite unusual for a man of twenty-nine to be still living with his parents.

Eventually, though, love had found its way to him, in the shape of a slender, rather delicate-looking Bedworth girl named Elizabeth Randle. Elizabeth herself was nearly twenty-eight years of age, so possibly the thought of marriage to a very handsome William overrode the fact that he was deaf.

Deafness it seems was his only affliction, as he took his Elizabeth to the altar six months pregnant, registering himself on the wedding certificate as William Harrison Deeming. They moved into another of the little cottages in Roadway Bedworth, next door to stepmother Ann and his siblings. Three months later, Elizabeth gave birth to their first child, a daughter, who they christened Mary Ann.

Mary Ann was quickly followed in turn by two stillborn babies; then, just as quickly again, by a strong healthy boy they named John. Elizabeth was gutsy: although of slight build, she shouldered her responsibilities as best she could. But with two babies now, as well as her household chores, she was beginning to struggle.

William noticed how tired his young wife was becoming lately, and it worried him. He was realising more and more these days that Elizabeth wasn't cut out for this life, that she wasn't physically strong enough to be a miner's wife. Not that she'd had much of a choice in this mining village. Unless she'd married a man of means, of course, and the likelihood of that happening was nil. Without education, you were nothing. A dispensable piece of flotsam floating in a whirlpool of hopelessness.

Mining life at this time put you one step up from the gutter, and as his workmates said, ten steps nearer to hell. Even so, a man had to be grateful he had a job at all. Every one of them in this community was fighting for survival, the old as well as the young. And if you couldn't stay the course, you were finished. Elizabeth understood this, and it placed a huge burden on her tiny little shoulders.

But she was determined not to become one of life's failures. No way would she ever give up on her family.

'While them babbies are asleep, come and sit yersen down an' put your feet up on me lap fer five minutes,' William would often chide her, after coming in from his daily stint on the pit face.

And Elizabeth, needing no prompting, would flop down in the chair opposite to him, closing her eyes, as his strong supple fingers massaged her swollen ankles. Both of them were grateful for these few precious moments of relaxation, to revitalise their weary bodies.

'Do yer think I'm a good enough wife for you, William?' she asked enquiringly one day, during one of her more insecure moments. 'I do try hard yer know; it's just that I get so tired just lately.'

William smiled. He leant over to stroke her hair, feeling its fine silkiness as it slipped between his fingers.

'What's brought this on then?' he said, bending over to kiss the tips of her toes. 'Yer the best wife ever, me darlin', cos I know things ain't bin easy for yer. This life's tough, an' you've no more meat on yer than a sparrer, but you never complain.'

And with this, he pulled her over onto his lap, entwining their bodies in a tender, loving embrace.

'You'll do fer me, my gel,' he whispered softly. 'You'll do fer me.'

While William toiled away on his long, arduous shifts down the mine, Elizabeth struggled to do her chores.

All miners' wives had to do the same: every day for them, too, was also a hard one. But now for Elizabeth, with her fragile little body already weakened by pregnancies, the daily slog was becoming increasingly hard. And now, to make matters worse, she was pregnant again.

This time, however, things weren't going at all well for her. She felt sickly and weak in the mornings, retching till her stomach threatened to force itself into her throat. She hadn't experienced any morning sickness before, even with her stillborn babies.

But she couldn't relax; she still had to wash the clothes, which to her was a feat on its own. Lifting buckets up high to fill the copper made her back ache chronically. Then, of course, there was the house to clean, and fires to be kept going. Dragging those heavy buckets of coal to and fro took all the strength out of her too.

Fortunately, William filled most of them, but she couldn't ask any more of him. He already had enough to cope with, doing his soul-destroying stint at the mine each day. Then, of course, there was still the bath to get ready by the fire each night. Lugging buckets of hot water over to that didn't help either; neither did two demanding babies.

Still, other wives had to do it and so, she told herself, must she.

William was a worried man. He wished Elizabeth hadn't fallen pregnant again, especially so soon. She hadn't seemed to have fully recovered from the last birth yet. What though, he asked himself, could he have done about it? Him up above did the deciding in that department, and he had no choice in the matter. Each child, so they say, is a blessing from God.

There was only one other way that this coming baby could have been prevented. But the thought of him not loving his beautiful young wife, as they lay entwined together in their bed at night, was inconceivable; from both their points of view.

By the time Elizabeth's new confinement came to its expected end, instead of blooming, as was the usual for most mothers-to-be, Elizabeth was now only a shadow of her former self. The pregnancy had taken everything out of her, leaving her weak and lethargic. As she lay on her bed in the full throes of labour, she could do no more.

Totally exhausted and being urged on by both William and the midwife, she tried desperately to bring her child into the world.

But her frail, almost skeletal little body failed her, so her labour dragged on.

'You 'ave to push, Elizabeth,' William pleaded, as tears ran down his face, mingling with the shiny sweat on hers. 'Please try just a bit 'arder. Just a few more pushes, that's all it needs.'

Driven on by the anguish William was displaying, Elizabeth managed to muster up some strength from nowhere. And she put everything she'd got left into her next contraction.

Now at last the baby finally slid from her rigid body. Gazing down on the limp little body of her dead son, Elizabeth's own life slowly ebbed away, with a devastated, broken-hearted William clasping to his chest her fragile, now lifeless body.

On her death certificate it was to read: Exhaustion after childbirth.

A day later, William stared down into the coffin which lay open on the parlour table. The tiny face before him, framed with her golden hair, was serene in its beauty. Gone now were any signs of the stresses of a hard life. These had been replaced by a translucent smoothness, which reminded him of a china doll. She looked so at peace lying there, cradling her little boy in her arms. How he wished it was himself she held.

Stifling his sobs, and blinded by tears, he stroked the fine, silky hair as he'd done so many times before.

'Aw, Elizabeth,' he croaked brokenly, 'Why did you 'ave to leave me? 'Ow can I go on livin' with you gone? You were the reason I got up every morning; you were me life.'But, like his father before him, William didn't take too long about his mourning.

He was now in need of a new mother for his children.

He lay his beautiful 36-year-old Elizabeth to rest, on a cold wintry morning in January. Then married his second wife, Rosa Neale, another Bedworth girl, in the July of the same year. In the same church he'd married and buried Elizabeth.

On the day of her wedding, twenty-eight-year-old Rosa, who already had an eight-year-old illegitimate son of her own, was already one month pregnant with William's child.

All the new family went back to live in William's little terrace: flanked now, not only by his stepmother Ann and his siblings, but also on the other side by Rosa's family, the Neale's.

Rosa became an instant mother to Mary-Ann and John, and William accepted Rosa's son Thomas as his own. Eight months later, Rosa presented all the siblings with a baby stepbrother.

He was christened 'William Harrison', named after his father, who had dropped the 'Deeming' on his latest marriage certificate.

ROSA

Settling back down into life in Old Roadway was no hardship at all for Rosa. She'd spent most of her childhood in 'Cow and Hare' yard, which had been a much quieter place than the hustle and bustle of the 'Roadway', where her parents had brought her to at the age of fifteen years.

The Roadway too had its advantages. She already knew most of the inhabitants who lived around her. And, of course, it was being here that had brought her together with William. She'd always fancied William Harrison; what girl wouldn't? But he'd only had eyes at that time for his Elizabeth. This she'd been able to understand, as Elizabeth had been such a sweet person; also the perfect neighbour.

After Elizabeth had died, Rosa had immediately offered to help out. She could see William was struggling to cope, so it was the least she could do for her dead friend. But then, quite unintentionally, one thing had led to another. A man could only do without the pleasures of the flesh for so long. And in that department, she knew how to please him.

Yes: She had, she knew, made many mistakes in her life. Getting pregnant with Thomas had been one of them, though she loved the lad dearly. A warm, tactile person, she'd always been very loving, even as a child. Unfortunately though, when she grew up into adulthood, she couldn't seem to be able to differentiate between love and lust.

Shows of affection, to Rosa, made her feel both secure and wanted, and she returned them with great sincerity and trust; learning the hard way that her childlike ideals of life weren't reality, that not all men had the scruples she had.

Hence, Thomas had been conceived, and the non-committing father had disappeared over the horizon, leaving her in a situation that other single men didn't want to get involved in.

So, for the next eight years, she had given all her affections solely to her young son.

Her friendship with Elizabeth had meant a lot to her too. She herself had been totally devastated when Lizzie had died.

She hadn't intended to get emotionally involved with William. Only to help him pick up the pieces of his shattered life. And of course to comfort the children, whom she'd been like an auntie to since they were born. In time, though, two lonely people had realised they had much to give to each other, and their children.

She was sure Elizabeth was looking down on them with favour.

Unlike her predecessor, Rosa was a much stronger, more robust sort of girl. Handsome and healthy looking, her chubby face with its rosy red cheeks, she was just the opposite of Elizabeth's frail beauty.

She was a good worker too, and a good housekeeper; stretching the meagre food rations a long way. Which was a good job, because quickly following baby William had come my father Francis, followed by Betsy, Martha, then finally Abraham. All of them healthy thriving children, full of energy and mischief.

'I'll tan yer bloody arses if I catch 'old of yer' was a frequent expression heard coming from the open door of the little terrace, after a trying day.

Rosa coped easily enough with her daily workload, even though the seemingly endless piles of washing made her fingers raw; this being caused by the hard rubbing of the dirty clothes over the rough surface of the washboard. Then came the cleaning, patching of the clothes, and cooking meals to fill the bellies of her ever-increasing brood. This took up the rest of her time.

None of these every-day tasks, however, held any real horrors for her. She worked with gusto to provide a strong family unit for them all, pleased at last to have a participating father for Thomas.

I myself only remember what my grandmother Rosa looked like from seeing a large head-and-shoulders photograph of her. This portrait hung in its frame for years and years over the mantelpiece in our dining room. Some of my older brothers and sisters had known her when they were children, and said she was affable, sunny natured, and humorous. Also, well liked by the locals, who she enjoyed having a good gossip with on a regular basis.

MY FATHER

As a small boy, my father Francis, or Frank as he was known, watched and listened to all that went on around him, taking on board that poverty, sickness, grief, and death was a normal part of life in this community. He had also witnessed happiness, humour and a very strong community spirit. Also, the never-failing will to survive, even when the odds were stacked against them. And from all this, he had learnt a lot

He knew the mine was to be his destiny, although it certainly didn't appeal. He'd often heard his father talking about the gaffers and the deputies, who ran the show underground. How relentless they were when it came to retrieving the 'Black Gold'.

He'd also been told how, if a man couldn't work, whether it was because of an illness or some injury, he could be ordered together with his wife and children to vacate his pit house, because, with no wages coming in, no rent could be paid. In some extreme cases the workhouse became the only option for the poor wretches.

He knew only too well that only the very lucky found other jobs. Usually, these were people with education, mostly from more affluent backgrounds. Very few miners were literate at this time. Even his parents couldn't read or write, signing everything with a cross

Now things around here were getting better, though. Schooling was at last becoming compulsory. At least now he might have some sort of a chance to better himself. That's, of course, if he had the brain and worked hard at his lessons.

So, full of determination, for the next few years he gave it his all. He didn't bunk off school like most of the others did; ignoring his pals when they ribbed him for being a swot. He became obsessed with his learning, but was brought down to earth each night, doing the numerous chores his father set both he and his siblings.

Even though times were still hard for them, now that his brothers Thomas and William were working down the pit as well as his father, their combined efforts were bringing in some more much-needed money. Their meagre wages, added to their father's wage, meant at least they had a secure roof over their heads; for the time being, anyway.

Next year would be even better, as he himself would be working as well.

As always, though, all good things must come to an end. In the year 1878, when my father was fourteen years old, tragedy again struck the family: another pit accident, resulting in the death of my grandfather William, at the age of 48 years.

According to the local newspaper of this time (I have a copy of this article too, and this is the actual recorded statement below).

At William's inquest, when being questioned by the coroner, the first witness spoke of the events of the day.

'I was actin' on the day, yer 'onour, as onsetter at the bottom of "Winnings pit, Hawkesbury". The deceased was abart to come up, as he'd finished 'is stint.

He got into the cage abart 'alf past six, and I gives the signal miself to draw 'im and another bloke up to the surface

Now there is two landin's at the top of the shaft, with six feet between 'em. At night, we reckon on using the bottom landin', and in the day, the top one.

On this occasion, when they got to the bottom landing, the banksman John Twigger stood there and he told 'em to stand still.

This meant they must go up to the other landin', cos the men goin' darn in the other cage 'adn't yet reached the bottom.

It's customary, sir, that when the other men do reach the bottom of the shaft, for the bottom onsetter ter signal they've landed.

On this day, the banksman, 'avin' 'eard me signal, hooted to the engineman to lower the deceased darn agen to the lower landin'.

Suddenly, it seems William 'Arrison made a move to get art on the top landin'. But the bloke in with 'im cautioned 'im to stand still.

But then, when they got wi'in three foot of the lower landin', 'Arrison attempted to get art the cage agen.

I hooted immediately; but it were too late, he were crushed between the two cages.

I miself grabbed hold of im to stop 'im fallin' darn the shaft.

He wus still alive, so I carried 'im into the engine room an' laid 'im on the floor.
He looked up at me and said, "Oh dear", then just died.'

The verdict the jury had returned was 'Accidental Death', probably caused by the fact that the deceased was deaf, therefore making it possible he hadn't heard the signals properly.

My grandmother Rosa was absolutely devastated, as were the children. It was yet again another cruel blow to the Harrison family. Our past history was once more repeating itself all over again.

Father was later to recall to me the terrible distress it caused him, seeing his father's body brought home in a coal cart, pulled by two pit horses.

This latest blow to the family simmered constantly in my father's mind, his grief shrouding over him like a blanket. But it also strengthened his resolution to get a better job, even though he'd been working down the charity pit at Collycroft, Bedworth, for some time. Meanwhile, Rosa could at least seek some solace in the fact she still had the boys bringing in a much-needed wage.

It is unclear at this stage why she decided to move house from Roadway to Hartops Yard, one of the many little yards that branched off like rabbit warrens from the main streets of Bedworth, taking all of the eight children with her. Whether her circumstances had improved or been reduced, I do not know. But it was while living here that my father had met my mother Emma.

DREAMS

My mother Emma Walker, as a young woman, was a petite wiry girl, with long brown hair, which was tied back most of the time from her small oval face, giving her a childlike look that belied her real age, and also giving everyone else a good view of her stunning pale blue eyes. Her great sense of humour was shown in the fine crinkly laughter lines that gathered around the corners of her eyes, and her small, but well-defined mouth.

Having the friendliest of natures, Emma was an extremely popular girl with many friends. And although quite small she was a tough little character and very adaptable. These desirable attributes hadn't gone unnoticed by Frank Harrison. But being attracted to this bright bubbly girl was the easy bit.

Trying to woo her, though, was a different matter; Frank having to run the gauntlet of all her other admirers first. But in the end, thank goodness, persistence paid off, and he gained his prize.

Soon they were inseparable: Emma constantly listening to, and encouraging, his dreams and ambitions for the future, while also keeping both their feet firmly on the ground.

'I don't want to spend the rest of me life working on that bloody pit face, Emm,' he said to her forlornly one day. 'I lost both me dad and me grandad darn there, and a lot of me workmates an' all.

The misery and heartache it caused to their women folk was painful to watch. Not ter mention the poverty it's brought to most of 'em.

Me mam was lucky, if you can call it that. She 'ad sons old enough to be workin', others didn't. I don't want to see yer in that same situation, Emma; I want things to be better for you. I want yer to 'ave peace of mind; I don't want you forever dreadin' that knock on the door.'

He placed his head in his hands before continuing on: 'But, maybe I'm just dreamin', like most of the other poor buggers I work wi'.

34

We all want out of that hell-hole, but will we ever achieve it?'

Quickly sliding her arms around his neck, Emma responded positively to his sombre words. 'You're not a dreamer, Frank, cos yer resolution to better yoursen never wavers. You study yer books every minute you can, pushin' yoursen too 'ard at times, wi' yer pit shift as well.

I know it's in the lap of the gods what anyone can achieve in their lifetime, but you at least have the drive to try. You can do it, Frank, I know yer can. And you know I'll always support yer as much as I possibly can.'

Frank took her gently into his arms, her words salving the horrible images of his father's early death that flooded through his mind. Burying his face into the softness of her neck, his anxieties quickly melted away.

'You know, we'll make a great team, you and me, Emma Walker, a great team. Cos I love you very much, you know, and you give me the strength I need to succeed.'

Frank married his beloved Emma in Exhall parish church, Coventry, the local Bedworth church, where all his ancestors had taken their vows, being under repair at the time.

Emma's parents, John and Ann Walker, were sorry to lose from their home this girl who stood at the altar resplendent in her simple white dress, her face as beautiful and fresh looking as the bouquet of lilies and roses she carried in her hands. She had brought sunshine into their lives, from the day she was born. But, seeing the look of love she transmitted to the man at the altar beside her as she spoke her wedding vows, told the wistful parents that this indeed was a marriage made in heaven.

This good man would love and look after their daughter always, and they accepted that their loss was his gain.

The young couple went to live in a tiny cottage in Industry Yard, Bedworth, or 'Dusty Yard', as it was known by the other inhabitants. Ironically, it was named after the House of Industry, or the workhouse as it was better known, which stood close by. Menacing in its presence, but now empty and derelict, its entirety was shrouded by neglect and desolation

Even in my own mind as a child, its reputation lived on. I had heard all the stories of life in the workhouse, many of them probably exaggerated over the years. But I knew it wasn't a happy place, and that people had feared it. On my visits to Bedworth town, as I grew up, I always tried to avoid looking at this place of past misery. But my eyes would always be drawn back, time and time again, to this intimidating building, which had the power to send cold shivers down my spine each time I passed by it.

If I gazed up into its blackness, and let my imagination run wild, I swear I could hear the voices of a hundred despairing souls, echoing from every nook and cranny of its sombre interior. This was the place where, years before, my great grandmother Elizabeth had nearly ended up. But now, thankfully, this one had closed its doors forever.

It was within the walls of their sparsely furnished little cottage in Dusty Yard that father made his decision to leave the Charity Pit. He spoke one day to my mother about it.

'Emma, if I'm goin' to make a move, I've decided I 'ave to do it now,' he said. 'It'll mean us puttin' up with a bit of 'ardship for a while. But I have to do it while I'm still young, and before any babbies come along.'

Emma nodded to him in agreement; she knew that his timing was right. She so much wanted to start having babies, but knew herself that this wasn't a good idea at this time. And she supposed, deep down, she should be grateful she hadn't already fallen pregnant.

So, in 1889, Frank joined the Griff Colliery Company, and was given the chance to sit for a mining degree. At last his dedication to his school work was paying off. He still studied every moment he could, even in bed at night. Books were strewn randomly in untidy piles around the tiny little bedroom which contained only a bed, with an old wooden box at its side – a makeshift table to place the candle on. Here, father would read and read, always thirsty to learn more; drinking in every scrap of mining knowledge his brain could capacitate.

Often, he would fall asleep when exhaustion took over, his books and papers lying in disarray on his chest, which mother would gently remove before blowing out the candle.

Things were very hard for them at this time, as Frank was unable to do a full shift at the mine and have enough studying time to pass his exams. This reduction in work meant much less money coming into the home. He himself was finding it hard enough to concentrate on his bookwork after his stint at the pit. The labouring seemed to drain both his body and his brain. Shortage of money was also becoming a worry, as they still had to eat and pay the rent.

Emma never complained about things, but this still didn't stop him from feeling guilty about the quality of life he was imposing on her. So they lived from day to day as best they could. They'd both known from the start that things wouldn't be easy. But neither of them had realised just how tough things would be.

Fortunately for them, they had underestimated the loyalty of their families, who rallied together as best they could to bring the occasional meal to the struggling couple's table; being as supportive as they could, even though they too had a job making ends meet at times.

Eventually, my father got his just reward: he was awarded a first class degree in practical mining, and was appointed overseer at Griff Number 5 pit, which was also known as the Metz. Then, when this shaft closed down at a later date, he was moved on to Griff Number 4.

His endless dream to better the lives of the Harrisons was at last becoming reality; life for Frank was changing fast.

A BETTER LIFE

During this exciting time for my parents, Emma became pregnant with her first child, and both of them were ecstatic about it. As they lay in bed on the evening of the day it was officially confirmed, father scooped Emma into his arms. Then, tracing the outline of her lips with his finger, he spoke tenderly, his voice full of emotion.

'I could never have achieved all I have, Emm, if you and our families hadn't been there for me constantly. I'll never forget what you've all done fer me over these last months. You've been me rock.

An' now, to cap it all, your givin' me the icin' on the cake, a babby. I'll make it up to you for the sacrifices you've 'ad to make on my behalf, I promise you.'

Emma kissed him gently on his cheek before answering him, pushing back a stray lock of hair that had fallen across his forehead.

'Frank, you owe me nothing. Nobody's sacrificed more than you 'ave to bring this all abart. Remember, any successes in your life will be my successes, any failures my failures too. There's nothin' so sure that we'll 'ave our ups and darns. But we'll see 'em through together, that's all I ask.'

Later that night, after Emma had fallen asleep, father lay pondering. This child, he told himself, would be born into a better world. It wouldn't suffer the hardships its forebears had; he'd see to that.

As she blossomed through her pregnancy, Emma could hardly wait to fulfil her own ambition, to be a mother.

Life had been very hard while Frank was studying for his exams. With little money coming in, she'd been pleased no babies had come along at that time. The house was so tiny, there was barely room for two, let alone three. Hopefully, now things were about to change for the better.

With Frank's new position, he'd been offered a deputy's house, one of the slightly larger of the 50 little terraced houses that had recently been built in Bermuda village by the coal board. Just the place to await the birth of a new baby.

When her time eventually came, Granny Mockford, the local midwife, was called for to deliver her. Everything went to plan: and the culmination of her pain-wracked body was a healthy little baby girl.

In her later years, she spoke to me about the birth.'It were the thing I most wanted in life, Mercia, motherhood.I hoped it wouldn't come too soon, though, because of the circumstances, wi' yer dad studying for his degree. But it didn't stop me longing for that time to come, and, when I found out I was pregnant, I was ecstatic.

When Granny Mockford handed me over the tiny bundle, and I put her to me breast, I sobbed me 'eart out. The tears ran darn me face all over 'er, I was so happy.'

Father was also thrilled to bits: he strode into the bedroom, beaming from ear to ear.

Taking the baby from her mother's arms, he cradled her to him, smiling as the tiny little face nuzzled itself into the roughness of his shirt. 'Oh, Emm, she's such a lovely little babby, and she's the spittin' image of you,' he said.

'I was wonderin': how do you feel abart naming her after our mothers?'

So it was decided there and then, she would be called 'Rosa Ann Harrison.' And on this first night of her lying-in period, the proud new mother gently lifted the sleeping baby up beside her into the bed, this being normal practice in those days for both warmth and easy feeding. Feeling life couldn't be better, but exhausted from the birth, she soon slipped into a deep, contented sleep.

The next morning Emma awoke from her deep, revitalising slumber with a start. Daylight was streaming into the room, its brightness creating distorted patterns on the bedroom walls as it passed through the coarse open weave of the curtains. Struggling to clear the thick mists of sleep from her head, a sick feeling of foreboding filled her stomach.

Something was wrong. Why hadn't the baby cried to be fed in the night?

Turning quickly, she threw back the bedcovers and looked down in horror on the blue, limp body of her little daughter. Emma picked up and hugged the tiny form to her breast, rocking herself back and forth in her grief. Her low whimpering changed to loud screams, as she called hysterically for my father.

The baby's body was taken away from her inconsolable parents, while family and friends gathered around to offer their support.

They tried to instil into Emma that the mortality rate of children was very high in those days; that nearly every family suffered at some time or another, as she was suffering; that she wasn't the first mother or the last to accidentally smother her baby in the night. But, they said, life must go on, and hopefully she'd be pregnant again soon.

Emma was in deep shock, and couldn't really take in what they were saying to her. Nine months and five days she'd waited for this baby, and each day had seemed like an eternity. Every hour of every day had been bringing her closer to the thing she desired most in the world.

How she'd fantasised about this child before it was born, wondering whether it would have her bright blue eyes, or would it have the small slightly upturned nose of the Harrisons? Now it was all gone: their lovely little daughter, who'd looked exactly as she'd imagined, had been taken away from them, and it was all her fault. She wished she could lie down and die too.

Later that night, Frank and Emma sought solace in each other's arms. Looking dejectedly down into her pale sad face, Frank whispered to her softly. 'Remember, Emm, not so very long ago you said to me, Frank, we'll have our ups and darns, but as long as we're together we'll get by. No matter how much pain we're feelin' at this present time, gel, we 'ave to put this behind us. And then, hopefully, the Lord willin', you'll be pregnant again soon.'

And he was right: pregnant she was, three months later.

Father, in the meantime, had now settled well into his new mining career, with opportunities and responsibilities coming thick and fast. These he handled with ability and enthusiasm, ever hopeful that at last his family could be leaving poverty behind them.

Keeping the men working under him focused on the job in hand hadn't been the easiest of tasks at the beginning. But once they'd got the measure of him, and he'd gained their respect, they buckled down and did a good day's work. They realised he wouldn't be a pushover, but didn't see him as a sadistic man.

Mother's new confinement was also going smoothly without complication, and both the parents-to-be were looking forward to the imminent birth.

When her time came, once again Granny Mockford was called for, and Emma gave birth to her first son, a bouncing healthy boy, who they named Thomas, after his great grandfather. Everyone was overjoyed: not only was Thomas thriving well, but also Frank had received news from his bosses that they were going to sink a new pit shaft at Griff.

A new shaft that would be named 'Clara', after one of the mine owner's daughters. And they wanted father to be the new underground manager. Not only would he have a new status, but he'd be expected to move into the pit manager's house: a large Georgian residence situated in Bermuda Lane, just up the fields from Bermuda village.

For the present time, family life for the Harrisons was once again sweet.

Eventually, my parents moved into their new house, which was named 'The Pumps'. This was because the 'derricks' that held the pumps used for emptying flood water out of the mines stood near to it. This was a really exciting time for them, and they had a great time painting and decorating, sorting out where things would go, and how to spread out such a small amount of furniture in such a large house. They would, they decided, have to buy more things later, as they could afford them.

Mother's fingers were sore from all the curtain making and cleaning. Everyone else who had lent a hand was feeling fatigued too, but had to agree it was a good job done. The old house was already getting a welcoming feel to it.

Father was busy trying to implement new ideas into his new job too. Mine managers in those days held high status and influence in the community, holding the responsibility of the miners' livelihoods in their hands. Some managers had taken advantage of this position in the past though, abusing the men by being uncompromising, even brutal. These tactics angered my father, as there were other ways to get the job done, without resorting to these methods.

He'd found out for himself how past members of his own family had suffered under the regime of these tyrants. He'd worked under a few of them himself, when he was younger. And because of this, he told himself, he would be firm but fair, and never forget his roots.

These new rules he set himself, he stuck to. If a man was off work genuinely sick and had no wages coming in at the end of each week, then he knew he'd only to ask 'Gaffer Harrison' for help, and he'd get it. But, on the other hand, Frank was not a soft touch either. He believed in a fair day's work for a fair day's pay. Woe betide any man who would deliberately stay away from work through idleness, placing his family in poverty and putting extra strain on his already stretched work mates. These men he would tell to buck their ideas up, or face the sack. He'd experienced these types himself in the past, when he'd worked on the face.

Often, after a sacking had occurred, usually the same evening, there would come a 'tap, tapping' on the front door of our home; and standing on the doorstep would be the wife of the man in question.

'Gaffer 'Arrison, please would yer consider givin' me man another chance? The babbies'll go 'ungry an' we'll lose the roof over our 'eads if there's no money comin' in.'

Very often tearful, and always nervous, they would plead their cases. And more times than not, father would give her man another chance for the wife's sake, though it would be only on his own terms.

He would never even consider giving the man his old job back. Instead, he'd give him a more menial one with less pay, working him together with other lazy or bad timekeepers. This strategy worked well: fed up with working harder for less pay, these men soon realised how much better off they'd been before, and buckled down.

Then, once the man had proved his worth again, he'd be moved back to a better job; Frank's angry words ringing in his ears.

'You ever give me any more trouble, an' yer out fer good.'

Yes, he certainly was a fair man, but he was firm.

AS THE YEARS ROLL BY

Family life at the 'Pumps' became more hectic as time passed by. Frank joined more and more committees, socially and with his work.

Mother was always on the go these days too, as, after the uneventful birth of Thomas, he had quickly been followed by two more siblings: another son they'd named Francis Alexander, and a daughter, Mabel. And now, just as quickly, she found herself pregnant again.

This confinement was also running smoothly: no morning sickness or other maladies. Small but strong and capable, even with three young children, she ran the large house efficiently, cooking, cleaning, and washing, with no outside help.

One washday, when she was in her seventh month of this latest pregnancy, mother set about the job in hand. First, she lit the fire under the copper to get the water nice and hot for the linen.

Later, after a long pounding of the washing in the dolly tub, she scrubbed Frank's dirtier pit clothes on the washboard. And then, after the clothes were all rinsed and mangled, they were at last ready to be hung out to dry.

This all took at least a couple of hours hard sweat. So the prospect of a nice cup of tea to lubricate her very parched throat was very appealing.

Checking that the children were keeping out of mischief, she went out into the orchard with her heavy basketful of wet washing. Then, after pegging out each garment in turn onto the clothes line, she paused and stepped back to watch it flapping in the breeze.

Pleased with her morning's efforts, she spoke out loudly to herself.

'Well, I'm really glad to see the back of you washing. But I don't like the look of that moody sky over there. It looks to me like we'll be 'avin' some rain afore long.'

Turning, she then went back indoors, looking forward to that cup of tea, and a long-awaited sit down to rest her aching back.

About an hour later, the sound of thunder brought her quickly to her feet. The washing, she thought to herself. Damn and blast the weather, I must have dropped off to sleep.Grabbing the washing basket from the table, she quickly checked on her now sleeping children, then went swiftly outside to retrieve the nearly-dry washing.

'Good job I woke up when I did,' she chided herself loudly, 'or it'd be a hard mornin' wasted, that's fer sure.'

The wire clothes line stretched tautly from a fixing on the house wall. It then went across a clearing in the orchard, where it was attached the other end to the trunk of an old gnarled oak tree. This old timer stood there majestically, its twisted branches stretching out like elongated fingers in all directions.

Mother quickly unpegged each article in turn from the line as fast as she could. It wasn't raining yet, but she was nervous of thunderstorms. They always had frightened her, and she wanted to get back inside to the children as soon as possible. Even thinking about storms was sending chilling shudders running through her entire body.

Nearly finished, she bent down, dropping another garment into her basket. But, as she did so, she was suddenly aware of a loud sizzling above her head, which was quickly followed by a deafening, crackling sound.

Looking up, she was just in time to see a flickering zigzag of bright blue flame shoot across the entire length of the wire clothes line, losing itself in the branches of the old oak tree, setting the nearest ones on fire.

In a state of absolute terror, she ran indoors, scooped up the children, and shut them and herself into the under-stairs cupboard.

There, in total darkness, she trembled and sobbed, clutching her bewildered children to her until the storm had passed.

That night, she went into premature labour, her tiny, newborn son living only an hour.

I still remember vividly how, throughout my childhood, whenever there was a storm, mother would sit on the dark stairs with her apron covering her face.

THOMAS

This was not the last drama to befall my poor parents regarding the children. A few years before I was born, another tragedy had occurred.

One hot summer's day, Mother had been busy in the kitchen baking cakes and puddings, when she was interrupted by a loud banging on the front door. On opening up, she was greeted cheerfully by two of the young local lads from the village.

'Sorry to 'ave ter trouble yer, Missus,' said the sweaty-faced spokesman. 'But young Thomas art 'ere's bin accidentally kicked on the leg playin' football, and he's 'avin a bit of a job walkin' on it. We've carried 'im up here so he don't strain it any more.'

Thanking them gratefully, mother went outside to where Thomas was sitting on the yard wall. His face was a chalky white colour and was contorted with pain.

'What you bin up to now, our Tom?' she smiled across at him, carefully inspecting the blue and black discolouration of the appearing bruising.

'Better carry 'im inside, boys, an' put 'im on the sofa. Then I'll make you all a glass of ginger beer, as you all look like you could do wi' one. And after that's done, I'll attend to the wounded.'

Two more days passed by, and, despite rest, cold water bandages, and various ointments and potions, Thomas was still having a job walking on his bad leg. Father was beginning to feel anxious about him.

'Best get the doctor out, Emma, just to check there's no broken bones,' he said.

The doctor came to the house straight away, and he gave Tom a good examination. Then he quickly put everyone's mind at ease.

'Can't find any evidence here of anything being broken, but the leg is very inflamed and bruised. I just think it needs more time for the inner tissues to heal themselves properly.

Carry on with the compresses, rub in plenty of Arnica, and keep his weight off it as much as possible.'

Mother sighed deeply. 'That's easier said than done with this one, doctor. It's doin' his 'ead in lyin' on that sofa all day long. Like all twelve-year-olds, he thinks he's too big to be med to do as he's told.'

The doctor laughed. 'Tell you what, Emma, I'll have a pair of crutches sent over for him to use. They should get him mobile once again. But don't let him overdo things, and I'll come and see him again in a week's time.

Thomas quickly mastered the crutches, but was still in quite a lot of pain. Mother wasn't at all happy: she didn't like the colour the leg was going and raised her concerns again with the doctor. After his examination, he looked over the top of his glasses at Frank and Emma.

'To put your minds at rest, what I'm going to do now is to call in a couple of my colleagues to look at the lad. One's a specialist in this field, who will know much more than I do about this type of condition.Don't worry too much, he's a big, strong, healthy chap; he'll soon be back on his feet again.'

Unfortunately though, the specialist didn't share the doctor's optimism. Taking both parents on one side, he spoke to them in grave tones. 'I'm sorry to have to say this, but I'm not very happy at all with your son's leg. The tissues are not healing healthily; in fact, they are deteriorating fast. I'm afraid the leg at the moment is looking decidedly gangrenous.

I think you have to prepare yourselves for the likelihood that the leg will have to come off immediately to save the boy's life.'

Frank and Emma were both mortified. Their first-born surviving child, a fit, healthy boy who lived for playing sport.

How do you tell him he has to lose a leg, and how will he cope with the news? But they knew it had to be done, and done quickly.

Thomas didn't cope very well at all with the news, begging and pleading with his parents to find some alternative solution to the problem. This tore them both apart, as they knew there was none.

'There must be another way,' he sobbed, clinging to them both tightly.

'I wanner play football, I'm one of the best players fer me age; the teacher said so. I want ter play for a big club when I grow up. I want ter play fer Warwickshire.'

No matter how much Thomas fought with himself, both physically and mentally, he had no other option open to him. And It was agreed that the surgery had to be done, and soon. Also, that it would be best done in the boy's own home, facilities for this sort of thing being very limited in those days.

A large scrubbed table, and a pad of ether, said the surgeon. That was about the best you could do in these primitive times. At least the lad would be in familiar surroundings and amongst his family.

On the surgeon's instruction, it all had to be arranged very quickly. Thomas was placed on the back kitchen table, and his bad leg disinfected as best it could be. Then, being held down on all sides; he had to endure the agony of having his leg sawn off at the knee, the ether only partially numbing his excruciating pain.

Sister Mabel was to tell me all about it years later. She said she nearly passed out as his screams filled the whole of the house. But she still had to help with his dressings.

Thomas's amputated limb was buried behind the headstone of an unknown grave in Bedworth cemetery, as this was the usual custom at that time.

Sadly though, he didn't properly recover from his surgery, and died a few months later.

His poor mutilated body was buried in Coton Church cemetery, Nuneaton. My heartbroken parents never really got over this tragic death of their first-born son.

A few years later, when I was aged about seven, I sat on the toilet down the bottom of the garden, staring intently at the two crutches that had hung on the back of the privvy door for as long as I could remember.

Curiosity at last getting the better of me, I decided to take them down and have a go on them. Hopping unsteadily down the garden path, giggling to myself, I called to my mother to come out and watch me.

She came out all right: with a face contorted with both anger and pain. She then gave me one of the few 'hidings' I ever got from her.

'Now put them back where you got 'em from, an' don't ever touch 'em agen,' she shouted into my tear-streaked face.

Looking back, I suppose I must have caused her great distress, probably projecting images of Thomas that she was trying to move on from. But I was only an innocent child at the time who didn't know any better.

Both my parents were buried in the same grave as Thomas when they eventually died.

The Harrison Family.'(Mercia, front right.)

MY ARRIVAL

The years quickly rolled by for everyone living at the 'Pumps'. The house, which was surrounded by gardens, an orchard, and fields, stood adjacent to the rest of Bermuda village. It was a child's paradise, which was just as well, as it saw the arrival of seven more children: Jack, Marion, Norman, Ethel, Mona, Desmond, and finally myself, Mercia Emma. The whole house was filled with laughter, love and a deep sense of belonging.

Father had now become a member of Nuneaton council. They asked him to stand for the Liberals, but he didn't have the time. Mr Melly, the mayor of Nuneaton, and Povey Harper, from Astley castle, were both mine owners. They would come to our house both socially and to discuss business.

On one occasion, just after I was born, Mrs Melly came too, as she sometimes did. She took mother on one side to talk to her privately. She spoke quietly, her refined voice now taking on an unusually humble tone. 'Emma, you and I have been good friends for a very long time now, haven't we? So I feel I can open up to you, without causing you any offence.

You are very fortunate in having all your beautiful children, Emma, and they must be a great joy to you both. As you well know, I am still childless, through no fault of my own. And because of this situation, I feel unfulfilled and incomplete. So I have come here today to ask you to make a great sacrifice for me.

Although I know things are getting better for you, which I am very glad about, I also know that with your growing family, money must still be very tight. So would you possibly consider letting me adopt your new baby, Mercia. She'd want for nothing, and it would be one less for you to have to feed.'

Mother was totally stunned for a moment, hardly knowing what to say. She looked into the sad moist eyes that stared into hers, and felt a lump rising in her throat.

She felt a deep sorrow for this elegant, well-dressed woman, who had on the one hand everything, and on the other hand nothing. She herself could only imagine the emptiness of a childless marriage.

'I'm so very sorry, Mrs Melly,' she replied sadly. 'I only wish with all my heart that I could help you out; and you're right, it is still a struggle to manage. But if I had twenty babbies, I couldn't give one up. I just love 'em all too much.'

Happily, a year later, the Melly's adopted a son, who they named Travers, then later a little daughter.

Sadly though, when the Second World War came, Mr Melly's beautiful home and gardens, which later became one of Nuneaton's most beautiful assets, 'Riversley Park', was bombed. The house and several others in the vicinity were razed to the ground, killing many people, including Mr and Mrs Melly instantly. Fortunately, the children were now grown up and lived elsewhere.

My earliest recollections of my own life were, firstly, lying on a mat in front of the old kitchen range, watching my mother making pastry. My father then coming in and accidentally treading on my fingers with his hob-nailed pit boots, squashing one fingernail quite badly, which has grown deformed to this day.

The second thing I remember vividly was when I was a little older. Norman, my brother, came running into the house shouting for me; he was breathless and excited.

'Quick, Mercia, get up on me shoulders, there's sommat art 'ere you gotta see,' he gasped.

Duly obliging him, Norman then ran out of the house, with me clinging for dear life onto his capped head.

We ran up the hill behind the house, and on reaching the top, joined the rest of the family and several neighbours. We were all about to witness, in close-up, one of the most amazing sights we'd ever see.

It came and swept over our heads like a huge indescribable monster, causing mouths to drop open and exclamations of sheer disbelief. Its incredible bulk reflected hues of both silver and brilliant white, as the sunlight bathed it with dappled brightness.

I outstretched my arms skyward, trying to touch it. It was so low, it seemed to glide just above my fingertips. Like a huge paper submarine it floated in the sky, its immense shadow, blocking out the sunlight.

The eerie silence was now broken by the effortless 'chug

chugging' of its rear engines, as it passed right over us. On its near side, facing us, was written its name, 'Zeppelin'.

'Come back, come back,' I shouted to this disappearing spectre. ' I want to touch you, please let me touch you.'

It wasn't until I was older that it was explained to me what it actually was; how this huge airship, a recent German invention, was being used by our enemies in the then First World War. Listening with enthusiasm to the unfolding story, I was really enthralled by it all.

Apparently, unlike the aeroplane, the zeppelins were undetectable by our radar. So they had often managed to sneak into England at night. The Germans craftily painted the bottom half of the zeppelins black, thus making them harder to be picked out by our searchlights.

Starting out from Germany at dusk, and arriving in England under cover of darkness, they would immediately seek out our cities. These were easily spotted, as they were illuminated by their street lights; London being the biggest target sought. Once found, the Germans would drop their deadly cargo of bombs from the zeppelin, raining them down onto the sleeping, unsuspecting city below, before turning for home; arriving back in Germany by dawn.

'Well why didn't our aeroplanes fly out and catch 'em then?' I enquired of my tutor, intrigued by it all.

'Because in the early days of the war, they weren't fast enough,' I was told. 'But we did get them all later, when we got better planes.'

'We showed 'em the door then, did we?' I remarked with smug pride.

I still found it difficult to believe, or comprehend, the thought even; that inside that huge fabric-covered framework, which had flown over our heads so low that day, had been enemy soldiers armed with machine guns. They must have been very lucky to have escaped being shot down by our British guns. Obviously, something must have gone wrong with their mission that day, leaving them still in England, exposed, and vulnerable in daylight hours.

It was a truly spectacular sight for all that witnessed it.It was certainly a sight I'll never forget, that's for sure.

HOME SWEET HOME

As I grew up, I longed for the time when I'd be allowed to go to school or play down in the village with the local children, as some of my elder siblings did. But, meanwhile, I had to content myself with the house and its grounds. I really loved the place: it always held an air of mystery about it. Every day seemed to turn up something new to investigate, both inside the house and outside.

The 'Pumps' to me was a grand, welcoming old house. Time had been kind to mother and father over the last few years; and now, with several of my older siblings working down the mine, they had been able to afford some of the furnishings and trimmings this lovely house deserved.

The upper part of the house had five bedrooms and a proper bathroom, the latter being a real luxury, even if we did have to lug buckets of water up two flights of stairs to fill the bath. This again was another major task, so we were all more than pleased when, in later years, we were connected to a piped water supply.

The bedrooms consisted of three at the front of the house and two at the back. Two of the front ones were for us girls; the other one being mother and father's bedroom. Theirs was separated from ours by a tiny room, which we used as a closet to hang our clothes in. It also contained suitcases, numerous filled boxes, and various other junk. We were told not to touch the boxes, but frequently did when mother was out. We were attracted to all the feminine frippery from her past youth which she kept in them.

My favourites were an array of black, white, and beige ostrich feathers, which we girls used to dress up in. Prancing around the bedrooms, we'd pretend to be ladies of the music halls, adored by everyone. That's until the spell was broken by someone yelling, 'Quick, mam's comin', get everythin' back in the boxes before we get our backsides walloped.'

The boys' bedrooms were all at the back of the house, as was the bathroom. Leading us up to them was a magnificent mahogany staircase, its rich red banisters glowing with the rich patina of age and frequent use.

It was wider at the bottom, the steps going directly up to a first-floor landing. From this, another narrower set of stairs went up at a sideways angle, to a top landing, which was galleried, a large skylight in the ceiling above it giving much-needed light. You could look down over the galleried balcony, and see right down the stairwell to the hall below. It was a long way down to the bottom.

Each set of steps was edged with intricately carved spindles. These added greatly to its overall beauty. I once fell down the bottom set of stairs, running to retrieve a large teddy bear I'd dropped down them. Luckily, I was saved by Rover, our large Newfoundland dog, who was trying to have a peaceful nap at the bottom. He broke my fall, and probably saved me a few broken bones as well.

The stairs swept down into a long L-shaped passageway. This went from one end of the house to the other, with a middle door leading outside at the front. This hallway passed by the stairs, front parlour, and the dining room. It then turned left towards the back of the house, passing by two kitchens, a small room where dad hung the horse harnesses, and the pantry, finally coming to an end at the back door.

Brother Jack kept his motorbike, a 'Radco', in the smaller kitchen when he grew up; it was his pride and joy. He wouldn't even let a raindrop fall on it, if it could be avoided.

The dining room was at the front of the house, its windows overlooking a field. Under these windows stood a large sofa, which filled most of the wall. Next to this sofa, in the corner, was situated a tall pine cupboard in which Dad kept his guns and cartridges. We children were never allowed anywhere near it.

'If ever I catch any of yer as much as touchin' that door, I'll take me belt off and thrash yer,' he warned us. 'Cos all guns are very dangerous.'

Needless to say, none of us did go near it!

On the back wall of the dining room stood a very large floor-to-ceiling cupboard, in which mother used to keep her crockery and linen. And standing next to the cream-tiled fireplace in the alcove was the small organ which Mabel and Ethel used to regularly play: Ethel could also play the violin.

On the other side of the fireplace hung the old mahogany wall clock, the rich chestnut colouring of its case shiny from years of polishing. The clock's front was encased in glass, displaying its white enamelled face, embellished with finely painted roman numerals. The large brass pendulum hanging below swung effortlessly from side to side, creating a loud, crisp 'Tic Toc'. This rather doleful sound, which echoed around the walls, was noticeably eerie when the room was quiet.

Finally, in the centre of the room stood the dining table. We only ate in this room at weekends or on special occasions, most of the time using the larger kitchen. This larger kitchen was light and airy, having quite large windows, which overlooked the back gardens. These let in the sunshine, which cast its golden glow over everything inside, lighting up the red quarry floor tiles, which Mabel scrubbed every day.

Standing on one wall in the inglenook was the huge black range, on which all our food was cooked. This had two ovens situated one each side of an open fire. Over this fire hung the gadgets used for hanging the stew pots from; also a spit for roasting the joints of meat.

I can still close my eyes and conjure up the wonderful aromas that used to waft around that kitchen when Mabel or mother were cooking. We'd all sit round the old scrubbed pine table, savouring culinary delights such as salmon and parsley sauce. This was served up with tender little garden peas, courtesy of our vegetable garden, as all our veggies were.

Living on the edge of Sir Francis Newdigate's estate also had its perks. It was many a poor pheasant or partridge's downfall, to wander on to our front lawn.

'Be quiet, shut your traps a minute, will yer,' father would whisper, gently raising up the sash window to allow out his gun barrel, before blasting some unsuspecting fowl into oblivion. Hares and rabbits also followed the same pathway to the stew pot.

One of my father's favourite meals was 'jugged hare'. He would add to this delicacy, while it was cooking, a full bottle of red port wine. I didn't like hare very much – it had too strong a taste for my liking – but dad would insist I ate some of the gravy.

'Get some of that down yer neck, our Mercia,' he said, 'an' you'll be grow'd another inch by the morning.'

My brother Des nudged me in the ribs, whispering quietly in my ear. 'That's not gravy yer drinkin', yer know, it's blood, pure blood, that's why it's so red,' then waited for the possible reaction of my running out and throwing up, scowling when it didn't work.

'I don't care,' I retorted haughtily. 'Blood or gravy, if it makes me grow an inch, I'm up for it.'

A disgruntled Des hid his disappointment in another generous helping of mother's apple pie and custard. Drooping eyelids often followed this meal, as the port started to take its effect on us.

After Sunday lunch, if we were thirsty, father would sometimes say, 'Why go all the way darn ter the kitchen to drink wearter. Get yoursens darn the pantry an' put yer head under the barrel. A drop of ale will do you good, put some iron in yer.'

It certainly didn't do us any harm!

KILLING THE PIG

Each morning we would have a good fry up for breakfast. This consisted of eggs, bacon, tomatoes, fried bread and, when available, mushrooms. Each rasher of bacon was sliced from one of the large salted hams that were hanging in our pantry. Like most householders of the day, if you had room, you kept a pig for killing, fattening them up with anything edible you could get your hands on. Household waste, bran, potatoes, bread: this was all made up into a swill and boiled together in an old copper.

I really liked the pigs and often sat on the pigsty wall, leaning over to scratch the large bristly bodies that vied for my attention. Snuffling pink snouts wrinkled with ecstasy as my fingernails raked their ever-itchy skins.

When it came to the killing of them, though, I wasn't so brave. I would keep well out of the way, usually lying under my bed with my fingers stuck in my ears, so that I couldn't hear them squealing. Butcher Goud from the bullring at Coton, Nuneaton, would be called on to dispense with them.

Dressed in his white coat topped by a blue striped apron, he'd arrive to do the dastardly deed; watched by an intrigued, but slightly squeamish, family audience. After selecting the fattest pig, he would then proceed to dispense with it, hanging its firstly stunned body from the branch of the nearest tree, before slitting its throat and quickly catching the fast-draining blood into a bowl placed underneath. This was used later in the making of the black pudding. After this stage, I would venture out to watch from a distance the appalling, but at the same time fascinating, slitting from top to bottom of the carcase, then the removal of the large mass of glistening entrails.

Every part of the pig would be used; nothing at all wasted. The sides and legs were the bacon and hams, the head would be boiled to make brawn. Liver, kidneys, heart, and other bits of meat would be eaten separately, or minced up together to make faggots. This would be rolled into balls together with onions and seasoning. Each ball would then be wrapped in the fragile, lace-like inner skin of the pig, called the veil. This would help each faggot keep its shape while it cooked. The feet and the hocks would be cut off next: to be boiled in the stew pot with loads of onions. These would make at least three meals for us. The intestines were put to one side for the time being. These would be used later to make the 'chitterlings', a kind of cooked meat. This to me was my most dreaded job concerning the killing of the pig. Finally, came the moment the boys were waiting for, the blowing up of the pig's bladder to make a football

After all this was done, the empty carcase of the pig was lowered down from the tree. It was now placed onto the embers of a fire burning below. This was done to singe off the bristly hairs from the skin, making it edible. During this process the pig's hooves would drop off the feet, sending us scrabbling into the ashes to retrieve one of these delicious morsels. These we sucked on enthusiastically, extracting every drop of its mouth-watering juices.

Mum used to say, 'There's nowt on a pig I can't use, except its squeak.'

All that was left to do now was to salt the carcase to preserve it, before taking it down to the pantry and placing it on the ever-cool block of stone we called the thrall. There was no such thing as a refrigerator in those days. I was scared to go into the pantry at night. To me, the pig's carcase lying there in the half-light resembled a corpse, and caused the hairs on the back of my neck to stand on end. So I soon fled the scene, legging it back to the sanctuary of my family.

The next day, the dreaded job had to be done; the making of the 'chitterlings'. This involved cleaning out the tubes of the intestines, which were still full of putrid digested and undigested food. A large pan of boiling water would be standing ready on the kitchen stove. Then Mother would bring in from the washhouse a bucket filled with the intestines she'd just boiled in the copper. Now we had to turn them all inside out.

'Grab this end, one of yer,' she'd ask of us, after turning out the first bit, ignoring our looks of revulsion, as the slimy, stinking contents of the tubes fell out into the bucket below. The smell was just horrific; it used to make me gag, intensifying as, one by one, the yards and yards of intestine were emptied.

Just touching them impregnated my hands with a stench which would take days to wash off.

Mabel would then use the boiling kettles of water from off the stove. Pouring the scalding contents down the now empty tubes; she'd wash them out, stretching each one as tautly as possible as she poured. This allowed the hot clear water to run easily down to my end, and into the bucket below me. Finally, after another boiling in the copper, the long, clean tubes, were plaited together thickly. We now had our 'chitterlings.' These were eaten cold, sliced off a piece at a time much like a cold meat.

I never fancied them myself, they still had that horrible smell, but all the others liked them.

OH HAPPY DAYS

The meadows around the house were heaven to me, especially on a hot summer's day. I loved to lie in the sweet-smelling grasses, my nostrils assailed with the fragrances of red and white clovers, vetches, and periwinkle. I'd close my eyes, and let the sun's warming rays beat gently down on my upturned face, listening to the sounds around me, feeling relaxed, almost in another world.

The beautiful song of the skylark hovering overhead was sweet music to anyone's ears, but was occasionally interrupted by the 'click, clicking' of the grasshopper, as he rubbed his back legs together, trying to attract a mate. I also liked to hear the 'buzzing' of the honey bees, as they flew from flower to flower, adding yet more pollen to already laden legs.

Everything is so magical when seen through the eyes of a child. The seasons, as they came and then passed, were always turning up something new. Nothing was more beautiful to me than when the usually unseen spiders' webs that graced the hedgerows were suddenly transformed, by the heavy autumn dew, into doilies of delicate beauty, each little strand of silk being covered in tiny droplets of water, resembling thousands upon thousands of little crystal beads: transparent vials of light that shimmered brightly in the early-morning sun.

Also delightful was the sight, after a hard hoar frost, of the tiny frozen particles of ice that covered everything around with a carpet of iridescent sparkle, looking to the observer's eye as if some unseen hand had sprinkled the landscape liberally with silver glitter.

Everything always seemed so tranquil and uncomplicated in those days: time stood still. This to me was what childhood was all about, and these times are my most treasured memories.

Sometimes, we children would go down to the big pond in the corner of our barn field. Then, lying on our bellies at its edge, we'd drop our hands into the cool clear water, making ripples with our fingers. There we would scour the bottom for newts, especially the males with their bright orange-spotted bellies. We would catch them and play with them for a minute or two, before slipping them back into the water.

We'd also watch, intrigued, the funny little caddis fly larvae, as it walked slowly along the bottom of the pool, carrying its home of vegetation and tiny stones on its back., Or watch the water spiders sitting in their watertight bubbles of air, which were anchored to the stems of pondweed by a woven mesh of silk. Our concentration would be broken occasionally by the plop of a fish raising itself from the water to retrieve a drowning fly, its silver scales brightly flashing as the sunlight reflected on them.

Other times we'd go down to the brook instead. Armed with fishing nets and jam jars, we'd try to catch the elusive little stickleback, or the large-headed bullies; returning home with bunches of catkins, pussy willow or elderflowers, depending on the time of year.

One Sunday, when I was out walking the fields alone, out of the corner of my eye I spotted movement in the hedgerow beside me. Scrambling swiftly down into the thorny undergrowth of the ditch, I was amazed to see a clutch of tiny yellow and black chicks, all huddled together for warmth.

''Ow on earth did you get all the way up here?' I whispered to them softly, hardly believing what I was now seeing. 'You poor little things: What's your stupid mother thinkin' of, bringing you all this way from the house? Dad will be really, really, cross if he thinks yer lost.'

Scooping up each fluffy little body in turn into my upturned apron, I slowly walked home with them, and, on entering the house flushed with excitement, I presented them to my father.

'Look here, dad. One of the bantams must have taken her babbies over the field and left them. But I brought 'em back, before the fox got 'em,' I said proudly.

Surprised, but very intrigued, Father gently peered into my apron, before folding up with mirth. 'Oh, our Mercia, what will you get up to next?' he chortled, wiping the tears from his eyes. 'These ain't bantams, gel, these are babby partridges. 'Ow on earth did yer manage to catch 'em? You'd better take 'em back quickly to where you found 'em from, before their mother misses 'em.'

So, back I had to go, this time red with embarrassment, to reunite them with some very anxious parents.

Another love of my life were the pit horses: big, beautiful shires, displaying thick silky leg feathering, which draped profusely over enormous hooves. These noble creatures, with their strong muscled necks, and powerful hindquarters, were used to pull the heavy wagons of coal by day. Then they were turned out to grass in the evenings, for a well-deserved rest.

Sometimes as many as twenty-two of them at a time would be grazing in our front field Outside our front gate was a huge circle of bare ground; this was where most of the horses stood together in the night.

If we'd all been out visiting, and returned home late in the dark, our sudden appearance would startle them. They would take off in full flight, galloping around the field, ancient instincts telling them to outrun a possible predator. On moonlit nights when this happened, they all looked like ghostly apparitions; the watery light reflecting silvery on their heaving sweaty flanks as they flashed by, their huge, thundering hooves echoing like drumbeats on the hard ground.

By morning they'd all be gone, taken by the colliers back to the mine for another day's work.

One early winter's morning, father drew back the curtains from his bedroom window. He gazed out on the blanket of deep snow that had been falling most of the night, transforming everything into a picture-postcard scenario. He also noted the horses, who were standing sensibly under the high hedges for shelter. Suddenly, his eyes were drawn to a dark shape partially covered in snow a short distance away from the others. Grabbing his coat from its peg behind the door, he went out, pausing by the boys' bedroom door as he passed, tapping it sharply.

'Get yoursens up straight away, lads,' he shouted. 'There's a hoss gone darn in the field, that's either dead or dyin'.'

Quickly he went out into the field, where he was soon joined by two of the older boys; and on them approaching the stricken animal, they were all pleased to see it was still alive. But with heavy laboured breathing, dilated nostrils, and its normally bright eyes dull and glassy.the horse hadn't even the strength to lift its head at their approach.

'Poor old fella; yer in a bit of a mess, ain't yer?' said father, stroking the horse's neck gently.

'Try to warm 'im up a bit, lads, while I go back to the 'ouse and make him up a remedy.'

Running back into the house, dad took from the pantry a full bottle of elderberry wine, which he emptied into a saucepan, then placed on the fire. To this, he added a large piece of crushed ginger root, and a quantity of brandy. These he simmered together until he was happy the root ginger was well infused. Carefully, he strained the cooling liquid back into the wine bottle, briefly cooling it a little more by submerging the vessel into cold water. Time, he knew, was of the essence, and was rapidly running out.

Returning to the field, he was pleased to see the boys had covered the horse over with hessian sacks. Squatting at its side, father gently lifted the horse's large head on to his knee, then slowly poured the contents of his bottle down its throat.

'It'll kill or cure you, old fella,' he said dejectedly. 'Cos there's now't so sure, if this don't work, you'll never see this afternoon.'

Luckily for the gelding it did work, and, with a bit of help, he was standing up within an hour; and, after a couple of weeks cosseting, he went on to make a full recovery.

'It's amazing what a drop of the 'ard stuff and a few herbs can do,' said dad.

We all owed so much to these huge animals, as without their help the miners' lives would have been so much harder. Their loyalty was always much appreciated by the men, who held them in high esteem. This went for the tough little pit ponies too. They were stabled underground nearly all their lives, pulling filled tubs of coal from one place to another on the pit face, never seeing the light of day until they retired, and by then they were often nearly blind.

THE DAILY ROUTINE

On school days we had to come home at dinner-time. We'd run as fast as we could, eat our meals, then run back again for the afternoon lessons. Woe betide us if we were late back at school.

At the weekends, we were all allocated different jobs to do. Uncle Tom Walker, mother's brother, would walk from Bedworth every Saturday morning to set us all on. And he didn't spare the rod!

My job, most of the time, was to clean out all the fowl pens, which I hated. After cleaning out the droppings, I had to fill all the nest boxes with fresh hay, emerging none too pleased back into the daylight, covered in fowl fleas.

One day Uncle Tom, unusually feeling a bit sorry for me, asked brother Des to do them instead; but Des, full of bravado, refused.

'There is no way that I am goin' in there with a load of fleas,' he protested indignantly, hands on hips.

This refusal was like a red rag to a bull, and was greeted with a good sharp clout around the ear, a purple-faced uncle exclaiming angrily, 'Get in that bloody pen now, you rousty little devil.' And in he had to go. We had a hundred hens at one time, so it was a big job.

We also had to collect the chamber pots, full of urine, from under our beds, emptying them all into buckets. These we carried downstairs to the garden, ready to be emptied on to father's prize onions.

The miners put on many produce shows in the summer months. But little did they know about the secret of dad's successful onions, which every year took first prize.

In the daytime we'd all use the 'privy' at the top of the garden. The latrine itself was built of brick and was quite deep. This was topped with a long wooden seat, with three holes cut in it. The stench of stale urine and faeces coming up from beneath you when you used it, was none too pleasant, especially on a hot summer's day. Not having the luxury of toilet rolls in those days, we'd all take turns cutting up newspapers, or any other paper available, into small squares. These were hung on a nail in the wall, next to the toilet seat. When I was older, I'd sit on the toilet with the door open, listening out for anyone coming up the garden path. If they did, I'd start whistling, just to let whoever it was know that the toilet was already occupied. This was a regular procedure, because there was no lock on the toilet door.

Once a week, men would come at night with a horse and cart to empty the latrine. The cart had a dish-shaped tank on top, with doors that closed after use. Our Jack, always the clown, would strike up in song after they'd left.

The moon shone on the shithouse door,
The candle had a fit,
Old king Cole fell darn the 'ole,
And swallowed a lump of shit.

The older boys had to dig and weed the garden at weekends too, once again officiated by Uncle Tom, who'd march up and down like a sergeant-major. We girls had to do most of the weekend housework. This gave Mabel a couple of days of well-deserved rest. She'd been kept at home after she left school to help mother run the house, and had sole charge of us younger children. She'd stand no nonsense, and would soon give us a backhander if we didn't toe the line.

At the end of the day, Uncle Tom would pull out of his pocket a bag of sweets. These he'd count out into small piles on the kitchen table.

'One fer you, and one fer you, and one fer your mother,' he'd say.

The sight of those sweets pacified many a sting from a clouted ear.

Even on school days we had to do our bit. Filling the coal buckets was the first job when we arrived home, followed by the collecting and washing of the eggs, the odd broody hen giving us a sharp peck on the hand, as we physically persuaded her to give up the contents of the nesting box. The lads would have to collect, saw, and chop up the branches of fallen trees which were stacked in the woodshed. This though, was more of a winter job, as obviously was the clearing of the snow off the paths and driveways.

We were all made to keep our bedrooms reasonably tidy too. This took the pressure off Mabel and mother a bit. Everybody in the house was given some sort of responsibility. Father thought it an essential part of growing up, and if you shirked it, you were in trouble.

Discipline was mostly administered by Uncle Tom or Mabel; father rarely smacked us, he only had to raise his voice. Mother could get irate at times though, when pushed too far.

SUNDAYS

My favourite day of the week had to be Sunday. After eating our lunch, we'd all await the arrival of visiting aunts, uncles, and cousins. Sometimes, the man in question would be Uncle Solomon, mother's eldest brother, who'd arrive with his quiet, rather plump wife, Harriet.

Uncle Sol made rather an imposing figure: with his large white walrus-type moustache, which was waxed at the ends into two sharp points, and his fat red cheeks spilling profusely over his stiffly starched shirt collar. When visiting us, he always wore a black silk top hat, which, when removed, revealed an ugly raised scar running across his forehead. This was a legacy left by an incident that had occurred a few years previously.

In the back garden of his cottage in Collycroft, Bedworth, Uncle Sol had converted a row of pigsties into dog kennels, because his son Frank wanted to breed bulldogs. One day, cousin Frank had to go out, so he asked his father to feed the dogs for him. This task Uncle Sol had done for his son many times before, so it was no problem to him.

Unfortunately though, on this occasion, after placing the feed bowls on the floor, a fight had broken out between two of the stud dogs. Within seconds, all hell had broken loose, as some of the other dogs joined in the affray.

Jaws locked on to scruffs and throats, causing blood to splatter over previously white coats: It was, I'm told, total mayhem. In desperation, Uncle Sol had waded into the pack, trying to kick them apart. But, in the intensity of the skirmish, he got knocked down and was badly bitten, needing many stitches in his forehead.

He was very lucky that day; he could have lost his life. Two of the dogs had to be put down, their injuries were so bad. What trigger had sparked off this isolated incident, nobody really knows. One possibility was that one of the bitches, about due to come into season, had caused the rivalry between the stud dogs. English bulldogs usually have such lovely, docile dispositions, so this totally out-of-character behaviour came as quite a shock to everyone. Fortunately, no problems occurred between the dogs after this.

Other regular Sunday visitors were Uncle Sam and his wife, Dinah. I was fascinated by Dinah: she was so stylish and glamorous, dressed up to the nines, loaded with jewellery, her long nails painted scarlet; she was sheer elegance. I used to think she must have been a film star before she met Uncle Sam, or perhaps royalty.

Dinah was such a contrast to mother, who wore long plain serviceable skirts and plain blouses. She rarely wore make-up, and the only jewellery adorning her red chapped hands was her wedding ring.

Sometimes, I'd sneak into the hall to retrieve Dinah's fox-fur stole from off the hallstand. This I'd throw around my shoulders, and gaze at my reflection in the mirror.

'When I grow up,' I vowed to the little face with the saucy smile, staring back at me, 'I'm gonna be like Aunt Dinah, and I'll marry a rich man, an' perhaps 'ave lots of servants to do me work.'

Uncle Samuel and Dinah had three daughters: all were very pretty.When they grew up, the eldest became a school teacher, the middle one a piano teacher. The youngest one was extremely pretty, her outstanding feature being a beautiful head of hair: long, bouncy tresses of waves and curls cascaded over her shoulders in a shower of gold. She went to work in a factory, and this was to be the worst decision she ever made. Leaning over her machinery one day, she got her beautiful hair caught up in it, and was completely scalped. It never grew back again: from then on she always had to wear a wig. It was such a tragic thing to happen to such a lovely looking girl.

Sunday evenings were also good fun. When all the visitors had gone home, the family would retire into the parlour. I loved this room, our 'posh' room, with its large, comfy, flocked velvet suite, that took up nearly a whole wall. The flickering wall lights, which had now been converted from candles to oil, threw a soft rosy glow through pink-tinted shades into the room and on to its contents.

A fire would be burning brightly in the grate, casting both light and shadow onto the large amount of brassware that stood in the hearth.

Against another wall stood mother's pride and joy: a spindly legged, glass-fronted Victorian sideboard, made of carved ebony. Its over-mantle was set with lots of small bevelled mirrors.

It was in this she kept her most precious bits and pieces.

The centre of the room was dominated by a round mahogany table, draped with a heavily fringed, green chenille cloth. On this table stood various family photos, set in silver or brass frames. This whole look of grandeur, pursued and nearly achieved by my mother, was somewhat marred by the long peaks on the bottom of this table cloth, which, instead of being green like the rest of the cloth, were now yellow.

This was caused by our two naughty Jack Russell terriers, who sneaked in and cocked their legs up it from time to time. Father was always really furious when this used to happen.

'If I catch them buggers in 'ere, I'll put me boot up their arses, and I'll put me boot up the buggers who let 'em in an' all,' he'd rant.

Pride of place went to the piano, this instrument being the hub of our Sunday social. This is what we looked forward to most: a good old sing-song.

Everybody would have a go, accompanied by Mabel, who's fingers would fly across the piano keys in full support. Father would be the last one to sing; puffing out his chest, he'd launch himself into a loud rendition of his favourite hymns.

'Into thy hands o lord we come', he'd croon, followed by

'rattle them keys, our Mabel; give it all you've got, gel'.

Some Sundays we would all be invited over to Astley Castle, in nearby Nuneaton. Father's friend Povey Harper, one of the mine owners, lived there, and I'd play with his daughters.

It was such a beautiful place, with acres of cleverly landscaped gardens. I loved to look around it. In one part of the castle was a huge domed area, topped by an enormous skylight. Through this the sunlight shone through, reflecting its light on the magnificent mosaic floor beneath. According to Povey, under this lovely floor was a deep well, which centuries before had been used to punish anyone who'd committed a serious crime. They were thrown from the skylight down into the well to a certain death. I never did find out, though, whether this was true, or whether he was just pulling my leg.

Mrs Harper was a very sickly person: she spent a lot of time in her bed, which overlooked the little church and churchyard of Astley.

When she died, Povey had her buried there, so he could look over to her grave as he lay in bed. This gave him comfort, as he was devoted to her.

He eventually got married again, sold the castle and moved away. I lost all contact with his girls after father retired.

FRIENDS IN BERMUDA

Now that I was at school, I was allowed to go down to the village to play, and I loved it.

My closest friends were the Fenton's, the Davis's, the Smith's, the Clay's, and the Elson's. Nearest to our house, just down the field, lived the Clay's, in the old gardener's cottage. Freddy Clay, my best friend's father, was a smallholder farmer. He had a field, two or three cows, two horses, and six children. The milk from the cows he sold to the villagers; also a few eggs from his hens.

It was to me a great way of life at the Clay's farm. Everyone in it had a laid-back approach to living. I found this relaxing, and very different from our 'A place for everythin', an everythin' in its place' house, as dad used to say. At the Clay's house there were no restrictions at all; it was great fun. The children, five girls and one boy, were often dirty, always scruffy, but were the best friends anyone could have. And mother couldn't keep us away from them.

'Don't you get goin' to them Clay's,' she'd lecture us, 'cos you're likely to catch diphtheria or summat else.'

Mona, Ethel and myself would often make our way down to them after school, then we'd all run riot. Up to ten kids at a time could be in the house playing. But this didn't seem to faze Mrs Clay at all. She'd always be sitting in front of the old range fire, reading the *Red Letter* magazine. Quite oblivious to the chaos going on around her, she'd be contentedly suckling her latest baby at her breast, humming happily to herself as she read.

Mrs Clay gave birth to a new baby about every eighteen months. It was nothing unusual, when we called in to see the girls, for her to plonk the baby in its pram, together with two full bottles of milk, then hand it over to us for the day. We'd then take it up the fields, playing mothers and fathers with it; making houses in the cornfields by flattening down small areas to make rooms.

The baby would be our baby: we'd play and feed it like a doll, returning it to its real mother later.Sometimes, though, we'd have to retreat quicker than we'd planned, when some red-faced, irate farmer descended down on us after seeing his flattened crop.

'I'll break your bloody necks for yer, if I catch yer,' he roared. But, luckily, he was never fast enough to carry out his threats.

Other times, we'd all play around in the farm dairy. Mr Clay, after milking the cows, would tip the fresh milk into a churn, then leave it in the dairy to cool. After he'd gone, we'd all sneak in to have a drink of it. Or we'd play milkmen, ladling it out into any other utensils we could find on the shelves, tipping it back into the churns when we'd finished.

One day, Mr Clay caught us out, and could see what we'd been up to. He had a really bad stammer, which got worse when he was stressed.

'Whaat yoou blinkin' lot dooin' in 'ere?' he stuttered angrily.

''Ave yoou bin drrinken my milk?'

A brave friend answered his question with the first thing that came into his head. 'No, Mr Clay, it weren't us, it were the puddy tats.'

'Weell then,' he replied testily, his face barely two inches from the terrified boy's, putting the fear of God into all of us, 'aall I can saay then, is there's some bbloody big uns in 'ere. An you aall know whaat I does to caats that steal me milk; so yoou better watch aart.'

Then, still cussing us loudly, he tipped us all outside.

Before he loaded his churns on to the cart for delivery, Mr Clay would often leave them standing outside his house, with the lids off. On a wet day, rain from off the roof used to drip into the milk.

Once I saw a worm floating in one of them. It must have been washed down from the roof by the rain. But as the saying goes, what the eye doesn't see, the heart doesn't grieve over. I could never quite work out though, how the worms got up on the roof in the first place. Perhaps the birds dropped them there.

On other occasions, we would opt to play in the washhouse. This was quite a dilapidated building, which wasn't as much used as it should have been. In the centre of this room stood a large tub of thick, grey, smelly, stagnant water: the putrid remains of a washday long gone. We used to play around in this water too. No wonder our mother used to worry about us catching something.

After all this fun, it would be back to the house, where Mrs Clay would still be reading the *Red Letter*.Meanwhile, Mr Clay would be trying, with great difficulty, to find space on the piled-up kitchen table to put his shaving mug and mirror on. He always had a shave before he went off delivering his milk. Often, when he'd had enough of us, we'd be all sent upstairs.

'Go on wii yer, uup them bllinken staairs out the road,' he'd grumble at us. We'd all run upstairs giggling together, either to make peg dolls, to play with the latest litter of kittens born on the bed, or just to chat; before letting ourselves down out of the bedroom window, when it was time to go home.

DICING WITH DEATH

It's a well-known fact that, if children can find some sort of mischief to get up to, they will; and we, of course, were no exception. Having such large areas to roam about in, and plenty of partners in crime to assist us, it didn't take long before we were doing something we shouldn't. And the thrill was doing it without being detected by the grown-ups.

The pumping station, from which our house got its name, was about an eighth of a mile from us. Large built-in boilers, about eight feet high, stood above ground level, and underneath each one was a firebox. It was the job of Mr Cox from Bermuda village to keep the fires going, heating the water in the large boilers to boiling point. The steam produced powered the pumps, which were used to empty out any unwanted water that threatened to flood the mine face.

Mr Cox had to check all the gauges on the top of each boiler to make sure they were up to temperature. Spurts of released steam would shoot high into the air when the pressure got too high. This relatively new technology was much welcomed, to help increase mine safety.

Sundays, when the mine was not in use, Mr Cox still had to keep the boilers going. He'd pop over early to fill the fireboxes with coal, then go home. Then, later in the day, he'd return to fill them all up again. When he'd gone home, a few of us would go up to the pumping station to play our favourite game of 'fish and chips'.

We'd collect, from nearby spoil heaps, large clinkers of burnt-out coal; these were our fish. The elongated leaves pulled from nearby elder bushes were our chips. Plates were made from pieces of broken slate that we found scattered around on the floor.

'Want some vinegar putting on yer chips, sir?' we'd all ask politely of each other. And if the answer was yes, we'd pull the handles down on the gauges, releasing the pressurised jets of steam.

''Ere ya are then, sir, your chips wi' vinegar.'

It was all great fun to us; though we could easily have been badly burnt by the scalding steam, we saw no danger.

Water pumped from the mine used to flow down deep underground channels. This water eventually finished up in a large above-ground reservoir. Dotted here and there above the route of these underground channels were large, high, circular inspection wells, which were built of brick. These had also held a great fascination for we children.

'Gi' us a bunt up ere, somebody,' was a frequent request from some scruffy urchin, his pants already minus a backside in them, his blackened knees covered in large scabs, courtesy of a previous adventure.

This was duly done, and, with knees gripping tightly to the brickwork rims, we'd all in turn gaze down over the edge into the murky depths below, the fear of falling down into this black abyss making us cling even tighter. The shaft itself could be up to a hundred feet deep, the water below just a small speck of silver. Dropping down our collection of stones one by one, we would listen intently for the distant splash, as each one met its goal. It was a miracle someone at some time never fell down one, but they didn't. Freddy Clay, if he had a cow give birth to a dead calf or a hen die for some unknown reason, would chuck the corpses down one of these inspection wells, to get rid of them.

Most of the Bermuda kids swam in the above-ground reservoir, as did Jack, Des, Marion, Mona and myself. The water came up to our shoulders in parts, although it was deeper or shallower in others.

We girls were told to swim away from the boys, or wait until they'd finished. This was because most of them swam naked, not many of them possessing a bathing suit. Sometimes we girls would hide behind the banks, watching them swim, giggling at the sight of their skinny nude bodies as they emerged from the freezing water, picking off the odd slimy leech. It was a good job Mabel didn't catch us out!

LIFE IN BERMUDA VILLAGE

The fifty little terraced houses in the centre of Bermuda village were all owned by the coal board. These were all separated off into blocks of five, each one having its own little back yard, on which stood a large water butt. This caught the rainwater from off each roof. Hanging on a nail by each back door was the oval tin bath used by all the family. Usually, especially in the winter, this was placed in front of the fire.

Every house had a tiny brick wash-house attached to it: these housed a sink and the washing copper, which sat in the top of a brick framework, a recess cut out in the bottom accommodating the fire. All the hot water was boiled up in this copper, for bathing and for washing the clothes.

Inside the main house was a small living/ dining room, with two steps leading down to a tiny basic kitchen. Upstairs were two tiny bedrooms, which sometimes had to accommodate families consisting of two parents and up to nine or ten children.

Over the yards were blocks of 'privy's' shared by several families. These the miners considered a great luxury; a big step up from the hole in the ground most families had used for generations. Behind these toilets were the allotments, where each miner grew his own vegetables. Wages being so poor, these helped to boost each family's meagre food rations.

In the middle of the village stood a shop that sold everything you could think of. I loved to savour the multitude of different aromas that permeated my nostrils whenever I entered it. These ranged from camphor and paraffin to mothballs, lavender bags, spices and scented sweets. I loved it when my mother shouted, 'Mercia, will you go down to the village and get me this and that?' because it meant a penny to spend.

On my arrival, Mr Betteridge, the shopkeeper, would scoop the flour, sugar, or whatever else I wanted, into his scales before emptying the required amount into a strong brown paper bag.

'Anything else you want, mi gel, or is that all fer now?' he'd ask pleasantly, wiping his floury hands down the front of his brown smock. This much-worn garment, threatening to burst at the seams, stretched over his ever-increasing bulk.

'Yes, Mr Betteridge,' I'd reply eagerly, 'a penny-worth of sweets, please.'

This was the best bit: my eyes would come out on stalks and my mouth fill with saliva. It threatened to overflow down the outside creases of my mouth, as I gazed at the array of goodies before me. Brown and white striped humbugs, aniseed balls, sugar fishes, pear drops, barley sugar twists, dolly mixtures, jelly babies . . . it was never ending. Pontefract cakes, liquorice allsorts, sugared almonds, sweets for coughs and colds, herbal tablets and Victory V's.

On this occasion I opted for the brightly coloured sherbet, which Mr Betteridge tipped into a small three-cornered bag. All the way home I dipped my wetted finger into it, sucking off the explosion of effervescent delight, arriving home with a brightly stained tongue and fingers that sported all the colours of the rainbow.

Other days, if my mother went with me, it would give me a chance to explore other areas of the shop, which were crammed to the ceiling in places. In the glass-fronted cabinets which stood amongst numerous other requisites were the pills and potions for every ailment. Fennings fever cures, Carters little liver pills, Gregory powders, sulphur and brimstone, Epsom salts, ginger, Wernett's headache powders, Beecham's powders, Indian brandy, castor oil, Vaseline and Zambuk ointment. Also Spanish liquorice, which you poured boiling water over, then drank the liquid to aid slovenly bowels.

Next to these, in the household section, was Acdo washing powder, Sunlight soap, Rinso starch, dolly blue bags, and donkey stones for scouring the front door steps; also Zebro black leading for the fire grates. Cherry blossom boot polish, Ponds face cream, steel hair curlers, and much more, were all placed together with brooms, mops, buckets and shovels In front of the counter were bins of flour, sugar, and hen corn. Also barrels containing vinegar and treacle, which Mr Betteridge would ladle out into your own receptacle. Alongside these stood earthenware bottles of dandelion and burdock pop, Tizer, and ginger beer; while hanging from the beams were hams and sides of bacon.

Finally, tucked behind the door, were skipping ropes, whips and tops, glass alleys with their beautiful designs in multi colours; together with five stones, shuttlecocks, chalks and slates, all these being bought for the children of the more well off. The local children made do with their own versions of these: a stick and a tin made a good drum. An old set of pram wheels and a box, a good truckie. A few even-sized pebbles, a set of five stones. There was plenty of chalk waste in the quarry to mark out a football or cricket pitch, or a hopscotch square too.

Life, with its compromises, was never dull in Bermuda village.

Clay's farm, though, was definitely the best place to play, as I've said before. Apart from the dairy, there were the hayricks and barns to play around in.

In one corner of Mr Clay's biggest barn was an old carriage. This elegantly constructed vehicle had seen in its heyday more affluent times. But now, the once plush, pink-quilted velvet of its upholstery was faded and streaked with droppings, courtesy of the many chickens that roosted in it each night. Ladies Mercia, Mona, and Ethel Harrison, together with Ladies Kath and Doris Elson, often rode out in this fine carriage, pulled by four imaginary white horses. We ignored the patched backside of our coachman, preferring to see gold and white livery instead.

'Drive on my man,' we instructed him, 'we 'ave to be back at the manor before it gets dark.'

Sometimes, in more sombre mood, we'd opt for the old 'hearse' instead. This too was in a sorry state: its once sparkling, beautifully etched windows now coated thickly with dust; the shiny, black lacquered paintwork of its exterior now cracked and peeling We'd all take it in turns to play the corpse, sometimes whitening our faces with flour to make the whole scenario more authentic.

Lying with arms crossed over our chests, a bunch of wild flowers clutched in our hands, we would take it in turns to meet our maker, escorted to heaven by much weeping and wailing, and a multi-choral rendering of the Lord's Prayer, ending with Doris's lament of 'We return our sister to the soil, from whence she came. Amen.'

CELEBRATIONS AND OUTINGS

Father still continually strived to make life easier for his miners. He oversaw that the pumps were well maintained, and that they pumped the water from the mine efficiently. He also made sure any other equipment, though sparse, was also in good repair. Most of all, he strove to keep the men's morale as high as possible under often trying conditions.

Every bonfire night, he was given permission by the mine owners to have a huge bonfire built on top of the hill next to the pumping station. Everyone who was concerned with the mine was invited to attend. He'd send up wagon loads of wood and waste coal, to make it a brilliant fire.

Excited miners' children, together with their parents, would come up from Bermuda, Bedworth, and Nuneaton. Out would come the homemade wine, barrels of ale, also pop for the children. Flames from the fire would reflect high into the black darkness of the sky, bathing everyone and everything around it in a fiery glow.

Roman candles, Catherine wheels, and many other sorts of firework exploded above us in a fantasy of colour and light, while jumping jacks crackled and fizzled on the ground, leaping into the crowd, chasing the excited spectators, who screamed with both fright and delight. Golden sparks showered from the stoked-up embers, looking like billions of tiny fireflies as they flew upwards into the sky.

For everyone watching it all unfold, it was an uplifting, magical scenario. People laughed, danced, sang, and drank, getting merrier and merrier as the evening progressed, stopping only to devour the large crispy potatoes that cooked below in the fire's ashes. It was such a wonderful time we all had on these occasions. The only bonfire my mother missed was in 1912, and that was because I was born the day before.

Some Sundays in the summer months, we'd go on a trip out in the governess cart pulled by our pony 'Polly'. Myself, together with one or two of my sisters or brothers, mother, and, of course, dad, who drove the pony and cart, would pack up a picnic basket and head for Cloudesley Bush, or Corley rocks, Both places were local beauty spots several miles from us, which seemed at the time a lifetime away.

Once there, we'd take a walk around the area, before settling down on the picnic blankets to eat our sandwiches and cake, swilled down with ginger beer or brown ale. Then we children would move away to play tag or hide and seek, while mother snoozed contentedly on a blanket, and father read his book.

Later, we'd make our way home in time for tea, throats sore from all the singing we'd done on the way back; Polly's shoes clip, clopping on the road, adding to the rhythm.

Each year, we had a special event, which all the local school-age children would look forward to each summer. The church committee would organise for us a Sunday school outing. They would contact Mr Clay at his farm, and ask if he would take the children out in his large 'brake' cart, with its rows of seats facing backwards. This was pulled by his two heavy horses, a black gelding named 'Satan' and a brown mare named 'Dinah'.

Picking up the children from the mission hall, he'd take us all out on a long drive. This cost our parents three pence each, the rest being subsidised by the church. On arriving back, Freddy Clay would stop off near the gates at the bottom of our field. Here he'd tip out the village children, to walk down to their homes below. Then he'd continue on up the hill to our house.

Then, after dropping us off at the top, he would drive onwards round the bend, before making the steep descent down the other side of the hill to his farm.

One such outing, though, went horribly wrong for a few of us. Returning from a trip with a happy band of travellers on board, Freddy disembarked the village children as usual. This left myself, his own daughter Dink, my brother Des, and another of his children on board. Just as he was about half way up our hill, an extremely loud bang went off at the side of us, possibly made by someone crow shooting in the next field. This caused his usually unflappable horses to panic, taking off at full gallop.

'Whoa, whoa,' shouted Freddie in desperation; 'hang on tight, you kids,' he roared.

He tried to reassure us, but his voice was drowned out by the thunderous noise of the horses' hooves, and the iron cartwheels grating on the hard surface. Fighting to regain control, Freddie was just as quickly thwarted by a sudden lurch of the cart, as a wheel hit a rut in the ground. He was catapulted sideways off the cart, temporarily knocking himself unconscious as he hit the ground. Seeing we'd lost our driver caused us to panic big time. We all started to cry hysterically.

'I want me mam,' I screamed to the wind. 'We're gonna die, we're gonna die.'

The horses headed for home; dark coats now glistening with sweat. White foam was beginning to form between their back legs as they plunged onwards. Clinging for dear life to our seats, we were thrown around like rag dolls, till every bone in our bodies ached.

I could feel the use draining from my fingers, and felt I couldn't hang on for much longer. Des's face at the side of me was chalky white, as was Dink's, the only colour in her face being black stripes, where tears had washed the dust away. I couldn't see the younger Clay girl. She was under the back seats; but I could hear her screaming.

Reaching the top of the hill, the horses galloped past our house and round the bend at the top. Mrs Clay, who at this time was quite oblivious to what was going on, had just come out of her cottage to put the baby in its pram, onto the lawn. Hearing a commotion behind her, Mrs Clay turned around just in time to see the driverless cart racing full belt down the hill towards her. The horses were going so fast, 'Satan' completely misjudged the width of the gateway, taking the left-hand gate off its hinges with the nearside cart shaft.

With either very quick thinking, or desperation, Mrs Clay whipped off her apron and flapped it up and down, as the terrified horses threatened to mow both her and the baby down.

'Whoa, whoa, whoa,' she screeched loudly at them, frantically waving the apron even faster. 'Steady up now, steady up.'

The sight of the flapping apron sent the horses skidding sideways, and they thankfully came to a halt just yards from the sleeping child. The two exhausted horses were no longer a danger to anyone, with heads hanging to the ground, sides heaving from all the exertion. The sweat ran in rivulets from their steaming bodies onto the grassy floor below them. They were completely burnt out, surrendering themselves willingly to the calming voice of the terrified woman that held on to their bridles.

Clutching at her throat, Mrs Clay hardly dare look in the back of the cart, but sobbed with relief when she saw the ashen faces of her own and Gaffer Harrison's children.

Taking us into her cottage, she washed our sore, blistered hands, and the dust from our red-eyed faces.

'Put the kettle on, mi gel,' she shouted to her eldest. 'Make some tea, an' put plenty a sugar and a drop a brandy in it. These kids er in severe shock.'

Anxiously she looked out of the window, sighing with relief as her gaze alighted on the staggering, mud-caked form of her husband.

'Thanks be to the Lord,' She whispered, crossing herself reverently.

The only funny side to this horrendous episode was told to us the next day. Apparently, the children from the village who'd been dropped off first had started to walk down to the village, when they were alerted by our screams. Running back to see what was going on, they had come across Freddie Clay lying prone on the cart track.

Their interest, though, was not in the fact he could be dead, but in the contents of his pockets, which were scattered around him. The sight of all those golden three-penny bits was too much to miss, so they'd grabbed one each, then legged it home. My mother never let us go in that cart again.

CHRISTMAS

The best time of all in our house without a doubt was Christmas. This was when the whole family got together; nobody stayed away. Preparations for the festivities had to be started weeks beforehand.

Plum puddings had to be made and boiled in the copper, each basin carefully wrapped in muslin, to protect its precious contents. Then the cake had to be made; mother's arms flailing the sides of the mixing bowl, whipping this delightful concoction of dried fruit, flour, spices and other numerous ingredients into a smooth, creamy consistency.

'It's time for us to make a wish now, mam,' we younger ones cried in unison.

Mother obediently handed us the spoon at this request, so we could all take turns to have our wish.

Eyes tightly closed, we'd stretch our vivid imaginations to the limit, conjuring up some magical gift that Father Christmas could bring down the chimney for us on Christmas Eve.

Mabel would start making her mince pies early on Christmas Eve; but she couldn't keep up with the demand, as the boys would eat them straight from the oven, before they even got to the table. Sometimes, she would still be baking them right up to the New Year.

Our next pleasurable job would be to make the house decorations. Many a pleasant evening was spent together as we made paper chains from brightly coloured strips of paper, gumming them together at the ends to make circles. These streamers we would cross over the ceilings in various designs. We would also make paper lanterns, and painted paper angels too.

Nearer the day, father would make an announcement at the breakfast table.

'After you've finished eatin' yer food, you young uns get yer 'ats and coats on.

We're goin' darn the field to fetch the holly and mistletoe this mornin'.'

So off we'd go, all muffled up against the biting wind. It was even better if it had been snowing, because dad would harness 'Polly' up to the sledge. We'd all pile on the top of it, scooping up handfuls of snow as we went along, making snowballs with which to bombard any unlucky sibling who happened to be off their guard.

After cutting off the berried holly from the hedges, it would be back to the orchard for the mistletoe. This parasitic plant grew in abundance in the nooks and crannies of the old apple tree branches.

'Come on 'ere, our Norman,' shouted dad. 'Shin up that tree; but watch you don't catch the arse of yer kegs on that twig behind you. Yer mother'll 'ave me guts for garters if you do!'

On returning home, we'd all help decorate the house. Mother would adorn the mantelpieces with garlands of holly, yew, pine cones, and ribbon. Bunches of mistletoe were hung from the beams, and the freshly chopped Christmas tree was put in its corner. We'd festoon this fine specimen with silver bows, home-made papier mâché stars painted in bright colours, and hand-carved wooden animals. After this we would attach tiny muslin bags filled with nuts or sweets; also little mandarin oranges, studded all over with cloves and tied around with brightly coloured ribbons. These cloves gave off a lovely pungent, spicy smell, which perfumed the room pleasantly. Another nice reminder that Christmas was nearly upon us. Finally, on the end of each branch of the tree, we'd clip on a small candle holder, each clinging to its own little candle

Overseeing all this work was the Christmas fairy: perched on the top of the tree, she looked so pretty, with her silver gossamer wings sparkling in the candlelight. Her hair was made of the softest yellow wool, tumbling over the bodice of her white muslin dress. Her little face, with its upturned, slightly crooked mouth, had dark lashed eyes of the brightest blue, all sewn on so neatly by Mabel.

Christmas Eve would arrive at last, and all the family would attend the service at our local church. Father was quite a religious man, and we younger ones had to attend Sunday School regularly.

The Christmas service was special though. I loved to hear the stories about the birth of baby Jesus; and everyone enjoyed singing the Christmas carols.

After church, when we arrived back home, we younger ones would be given a mug of cocoa, then sent to bed. But even though it was past our normal bedtime, sleep for us didn't come easily. Mona, Ethel, and myself, our hair spirally wound in rags to create ringlets, would lie in bed chatting with excitement, trying to pass the time away, hoping to catch a glimpse of Father Christmas.

'Let's sing some songs until he comes,' suggested Ethel, propping herself up on one elbow, before launching herself into a screeching rendition of 'The First Noel', Mona and myself joining in the chorus. This singing went on for another half an hour, before it was rudely interrupted by a loud banging on the back wall. This was closely followed by Jack's loud, bellowing voice proclaiming,

'If you bloody lot don't shut up, yer won't even live to see Christmas Day, any on yer. Some of us in 'ere are tryin' ter get some sleep.'

The hairs on Mona's arms visibly bristled, her lips pursing together with anger. Never being one to back down gracefully, she wasn't about to do so now.

'You just shut your mouth, our Jack,' she retorted angrily. We want to stay awake to listen for Father Christmas comin'.'

'Well, you can be rest assured he won't be comin' ere, if you keep on makin' that soddin' row; that's a certainty,' was Jack's final comment.

Christmas Day was here at last: eyes, blurry and tired through lack of sleep, were forced open and made to focus.

'He's bin, he's bin,' I squealed with delight, 'there's things in my stockin'.'

This brought everyone to their senses, all leaping out of bed to examine the hose suspended on the bottom bedsteads. Shrieks of excitement came from each of us, as we surveyed the contents of our stockings.

'Oh, wow! Look at this beautiful tortoiseshell hair slide,' gasped Marion, clipping it into the waves of her lovely thick hair, while Mona drooled over a pair of cream satin slippers, lovingly fingering the lace edging.

'What 'ave you got, Mercia? Let's have a look,' she asked dreamily.

'Oh I've got a rag dolly, a whip and top, a bag of sweets, two sugar mice, and an apple and an orange, and look, a new penny. Ain't I lucky,' I chanted in joyous rapture, twirling around the room, the rag doll swinging limply in my arms.

'Thank you very much, Father Christmas, for everythin' you've given us today.'

Soon the place was buzzing, as in came the boys to give us a showing of their presents too. Excited laughter filled the room as they did so.

Mabel came in soon after, bringing the jollity to an end.

'Come on you lot, into the bathroom wi' yer, get yoursens spotless, or I'll do it for yer with the scrubbing brush. You wash that filthy neck, our Des, an' try usin' soap for a change. I want all of yer dressed in your best bib an' tuckers, then darn them stairs for breakfast.'

Breakfast on Christmas Day was very light. Just a slice of toast and a cup of tea, leaving plenty of room in the stomach for Christmas dinner. Already, mother had the goose cooking slowly on the spit, its plump white breast swelled out further by her home-made sage and onion stuffing. We always had goose or suckling pig at Christmas, never turkey.

Meanwhile, white turnips, Brussels sprouts, carrots, peas, potatoes and parsnips all waited in saucepans ready for boiling or baking, while the goose's neck and gizzard simmered gently in the stockpot ready to make gravy.

Every year, Aunt Liz and Uncle Tom Walker would come from Bedworth for Christmas dinner. The scenario in the kitchen each year would be always the same. Aunt Liz would sit in the recess by the kitchen fire, a large white apron tied around her more than ample middle. She'd be basting the goose with its own sizzling fat, as it rotated slowly on the spit. At her side stood a small table, on which sat a more than generous glass of whisky. She'd sip at this constantly, chatting and laughing amiably, as she basted.

Auntie loved doing this job, her chubby face getting redder and redder as time went on. Until, as always, the effects from both the fire and the whisky sent her into a blissfully deep slumber.

One year, after she'd nodded off, brother Jack gently placed a white mouse in her apron pocket, covering it up with her handkerchief. When she woke up, she pulled out her hanky with the mouse in tow. Her hysterical screaming could be heard all over the house.

'It were 'im, I know it were 'im,' she fumed at our Jack. 'You little hellion, only you'd do a trick like that. I could 'ave had an 'eart attack, yer little bugger.'

Jack replied to her tirade sweetly, as always the picture of complete innocence.

'Weren't me, Aunt Liz. Why would you think fer one minute that I'd do a thing like that to me favourite auntie? No way.'

This comment made Aunt Liz madder than ever, her face turning purple with anger.

'You're a little liar, that's what you are, Jack Harrison, a little liar.' And with the full force of her rage, she brought her hand up sharply, clipping him hard round the back of his head.

'An' if you ever try that one on me agen, Christmas or no Christmas, I'll get yer Uncle Tom to whack yer arse till you can't sit darn.'

After a most delicious dinner, everyone sat themselves down in the parlour, all awaiting the arrival of other relatives and friends, and the older boys' girlfriends. We would then play all sorts of seasonal games together: blind man's buff, dominoes, card games, pass the parcel, and, of course, the inevitable sing-song, with Mabel as usual on the organ, and Ethel struggling to keep up on her violin.

Marion came abruptly into the room at one point, giggling behind her hand.

'Guess what! I've just seen our Frank kissing his Ethel under the mistletoe.'

Yes, Christmas was the happiest of times for us now. But father never let us be complacent. His memories of the not-too-distant past were still vivid in his mind.

'Thank the Lord for the blessin's he's bestowed on yer. But never forget the unfortunates that ain't so lucky. Always remember yer roots,' he told us.

NEW YEAR

After Christmas, everything went back to normal, and we all came down to reality. Father and the older boys went back to work at the mine, and we younger ones resumed school.

The long walk to the school and back kept us all healthy, but having to come home for lunch was a pain, especially if the weather was bad. The Bermuda children only had to walk back home to the village, but I had the long, steep walk up the fields to get to our house, often getting soaked to the skin in the process. My very best friend's mother often came to my rescue.

Mrs Fenton and her husband lived in one of the bottom cottages in the village; they were a family of eleven. Mrs Fenton would cook broth in the washing copper, she had so many mouths to feed. She was a big-hearted woman, was Mrs Fenton, and she spoke to my mother about my situation.

'If the weather's bad, Mrs 'Arrison, why don't I see ter Mercia's dinner? It'll save the wench trampsin' up them fields, getting wetter an' wetter. One more mouth to feed won't make much difference 'ere.'

I looked forward to those days, crammed in around that old rickety pine table, listening and responding to the happy chatter of the other children. Our bellies would be rumbling, and mouths drooling, as Mrs Fenton would ladle out the broth. This would be brimming with every type of vegetable imaginable, courtesy of my mother, who would insist she had them as a thank you token. These veggies must have made a great contribution to the feeding of the Fenton siblings. A case of you scratch my back, and I'll scratch yours.

Mrs Fenton was called by some of the other villagers 'The lady of the night'. She acquired this name because every Saturday night she always went out, usually to escape from the daily drudgery her large family inflicted on her. After her husband had finished his shift, bathed and been fed, a quite amazing transformation would take place in the front bedroom of the Fenton household. Off would come the scruffy grease-stained day clothes and the worn leather boots, with their broken laces. Also the old battered felt hat, which usually covered a mop of sometimes none-too-clean hair. On would go the full make-up, complete with bright red lips and rouged cheeks. High-heeled shoes, though slightly scuffed, complemented the slinky, figure-hugging dresses, which, to her credit, belied the fact she had birthed nine children. Then, with her hair freshly washed and teased into a poor representation of the latest style, she'd top it all off with a flash, though slightly moth-eaten, fox fur stole.

Leaving her children tucked up asleep in bed and her husband lying in his usual comatose position on the couch, snoring loudly, this now-transformed, 'Greta Garbo' style Mrs Fenton would totter out of the village, under cover of darkness, to Hill Top Nuneaton, where the then landlord of the Wharf Inn would repeatedly offer to show her a good time.

Only once did she come to grief, as far as I know: when she was chased by a herd of cows as she crossed a field on her way home at some unearthly time of night. Arriving home dishevilled, shoeless, and mud spattered, much to the amusement of vigilant neighbours.

The Fentons' eldest daughter, Kathleen, was my best friend. She was a lovely looking girl with the bluest eyes I've ever seen. Her hair was fair, but her lashes and eyebrows were jet black, emphasising her eyes even more. All of the members of the Fenton family were nice people.

As soon as possible in the New Year we would go down to the village to spend our Christmas pennies. But, instead of going to the big shop, we'd opt for the Cookson's. This older couple ran a sweet shop from the front room of their tiny pit house, and were more generous with the sweet rations than Mr Betteridge was.

I myself didn't really like going there. And, although the thought of extra sweets usually decided the issue, I was always a bit nervous. This was because, when you entered the shop, Mrs Cookson would be sitting by the fire, her face half-covered by her apron. Sometimes, though, she wasn't quick enough, and my eyes would be drawn reluctantly to the large disfiguring deformity that covered half her face, which I was a bit daunted by.

Poor Mrs Cookson. In hindsight, it must have distressed this gentle lady very much to know the local children found her a bit frightening.

Mr Cookson, though, had no such inhibitions. Sitting behind the table with the jars of sweets behind him, he'd beckon us towards him.

'Hello there, girls,' he'd say, in his usual charming, charismatic voice. 'Come on over 'ere an' pick what sweets you want.'

This we'd gladly do, but were careful to stand at the front of the table; this was after being pre-warned by other unfortunates.

'Don't get standin' too close to that dirty old bugger, cos he puts 'is 'ands up yer frock.'

Some other characters living in the village were the Acock's. Both these people were very tall, as was their daughter, Alice, who was about six foot four. Quite in contrast was Mrs Acock's sister, Nellie, who was a three-foot dwarf. It was quite comical to see them out together, Alice's height being more emphasised when walking hand in hand with her tiny Auntie Nellie. We were taught knitting, crochet, and sometimes cooking in the mission hall by the multi-talented Nellie.

Meanwhile, the lads all played football on the field behind. She was a lovely jolly little person was Nellie, who always wore flamboyant, colourful hats. Quite a dynamic person was tucked away in that little body.

There were three separate houses at the bottom of our field. These belonged to the Fry's, the Hazelwood's, and, further back, the Mockford's. Granny Mockford was the midwife; she delivered all the local babies, including myself. Her eldest daughter was the headmistress of my first school. Grandad Mockford, with his thick white beard, was the double of the old King George.

Near the Mockford's were more cottages, next to the railway gates. These housed the Starmer's, the Elsons's, and the Humphries, Mr Humphries being responsible for letting the trains in and out of the colliery.

It was a happy little community of people in Bermuda village, despite the poverty which surrounded most of the inhabitants of that time.

GEORGE

Doris Elson was another of my best friends: we were very close to each other. Doris and her two brothers lived with their parents down by the canal side. Her elder brother, George, was a quiet, happy boy, but was slightly mentally handicapped. He had the most beautiful tenor voice, which could often be heard at our house as it floated up from the cottage below.

One summer's day, Doris called round for me and we walked back down to the canal side. I loved to sit down on its grassy banks, watching the brightly coloured damsel flies skimming the top of its murky water. We threw pebbles at the small pieces of wood that were bobbing up and down on the ripples made by disappearing coal barges. Soon bored by this, we were more than happy at the arrival of George Elson. His mouth, set in a florid, rather sweaty face, broke into a sloppy, lopsided grin at the sight of us.

'Hey, you two' he shouted affably, lumbering over to greet us in his familiar rolling gait.

'There's a dead crow in the canal arm, do you wanna help me get it art?'

Needing no second invitation, we made our way over to the quiet backwater where the boats turned round. There, just as George had said, was a partially submerged crow, the sun shining on its glossy black feathers, reflecting on the iridescent hues of both green and blue. Try as we might, though, this poor sad creature remained well out of our reach Our frustrations were soon ended by the sound of Mrs Elson's shrill voice, calling her children in for tea.

'Better get yoursen 'ome too, Mercia' she shouted. 'Bet your mother's bin callin' you an' all.'

Scrambling up the bank, Doris paused to look back at George.

'Come on now, big fella, or there'll be nowt left on the table fer you,' she chided him in her usual motherly fashion, before running to catch up with me.

Later that evening, after we'd eaten, brother Frank came in from his shift at the pit.

'Sorry I'm late,' he excused himself, hanging his coat and cap behind the kitchen door, before sinking himself into a chair to remove his boots.

'Right bloody commotion goin' on darn the bottom,' he said, shaking his head from side to side.

'Poor George Elson has been drarned in the canal arm. Seems the silly bugger was proddin' a dead crow wi' a stick, overbalanced an' fell in. His dad found 'im, when he went to get 'im in for his tea. It's a terrible shame, cos he was a nice, harmless enough chap,' he said glumly.

Hearing this, I was mortified. It had obviously happened not long after Doris and I had left him behind. I felt sick inside, but daren't tell my mother as she didn't approve of us going too near to the canal.

I shed many tears that night for the inoffensive young man whose beautiful voice would never be heard again. Also for Doris and her parents, who I knew would be absolutely heartbroken.

The next day on the way to school I had to pass by the Elson's little cottage. Everything there seemed unnaturally silent. But what upset me the most was the sight of George's clothes spread over the gooseberry bushes to dry. These well-worn, but still useful articles would be handed down to George's younger brother. Nothing could be wasted; poverty dictated all.

This wasn't the only tragedy to befall the Elson's. A few years later, my best friend's mother embarked on an illicit love affair with the man next door. This gave all the village gossips plenty to chew on. Heads got together on a regular basis, eager to hear any juicy little snippets that would add flavour to the situation.

In the beginning, the illicit couple kept their liaison behind closed doors. But, as time went on, they became more brazen, flaunting their affair blatantly for all to see. This didn't go down at all well with most of the locals. The villagers' sympathies lay with the lady in question's husband. They thought this kind, gentle man didn't deserve the public humiliation he was getting. As feelings ran higher and higher, things got quickly out of hand. Small groups of scathing bystanders, banding together to form an ugly mob, decided to take matters into their own hands, forcibly dragging both my friend's mother and her boyfriend from their homes.

Picking up anything that made a noise, the miners drummed the frightened couple out of the village, showering them with sticks and small stones. Brother Des and myself, who were playing down in the village at that time, got caught up in all the excitement, and marched along noisily behind the crowd. The couple, terrified for their lives, never returned to the village again. Sadly, though, this scenario was to have the most tragic consequences, when the grieving husband, feeling he'd got nothing else to live for, hanged himself a few days later from his apple tree. I think he would rather have put up with the situation as it then was, than lose his wife completely, as he thought the world of her.

I don't think he'd ever fully recovered from the drowning of poor George, his eldest, much loved son. My friend and her younger brother were sent away to live with relatives. I missed her dreadfully. As for mine and Des's part in the drumming fiasco, Mabel found out about it and gave us both a good hiding.

'That'll teach yer to poke your nose into other people's business, won't it,' was the answer to our sore backsides.

THE EXPLOSION

One night, when I was about ten years old, the whole household was awoken from their slumbers by the most ominous sound a mining community could hear: the sound of the sirens and hooters going off at the mine. This wailing sound could mean only one thing: a pit disaster.

Pit accidents were not so common now, but still many lives were unnecessarily lost. Not many households remained untouched by grief. Father was still continually pressing for better safety measures, and things were much improved; but there was always the unexpected.

My parents quickly responded to the messenger who banged relentlessly on the front door and windows.

'Gaffer, gaffer,' he shouted, 'get up, there's bin an explosion below ground on the face.'

Both were up and dressed in minutes, hurrying downstairs and out into the darkness, Mother stopping briefly to exchange words with a startled Mabel, who was gazing down from the balcony above.

'Hold the fort will yer, Mabel? There's bin an explosion down on the face. Keep things as quiet as you can from the young uns, an' try not to worry yoursen. We'll keep you informed as best we can.'

Hope I can practice what I preach, she thought to herself, her heart beating rapidly inside her chest as she hurried outside. But it's not so easy when you've got two sons of your own working that shift.

The haunting wail of the sirens had brought the whole community from their beds. Scores of shadowy figures could be seen in the twilight, running towards the mine. Mothers, fathers and grandparents, some having sons, husbands, or fathers working the shift. Others just wanting to help out. All fearful as to what they would find when they reached their destination.

Arriving at the pit head, Father was briefed on the situation. The cause of the explosion was as yet unknown; most of the men had got out safely, but others were trapped underground. Rescue operations were already underway as brave miners dug through the debris, some with their bare hands. They thought little of the danger to themselves, risking all to save their workmates.

It was thought that the accident could have been triggered by a spark: possibly from a pick striking on hard coal. Or perhaps a spark from under the steel wheels of one of the coal wagons, as it came in contact with the underground railway line. Either of these could have ignited a pocket of methane gas, the deadly unseen by-product of the coal, which sometimes built up to dangerous levels underground. Whatever the cause, the explosion had brought down part of the tunnel roof, trapping miners underneath it. Fire had already broken out in parts of the tunnel too.

Brother Norman had been located now as safe, but brother Frank was still unaccounted for.

As the debris was slowly cleared away, it was removed in the coal wagons, as were the injured and dead. Sobs of relief from mothers of the wounded were drowned out by the wails of the mothers and wives of the dead, as they gazed, one by one, upon the crushed, lifeless bodies of their husbands and sons.

Mother frantically sought out my father.

'Any news yet, Frank?' she asked nervously, clutching at the lapels of his now mud-stained jacket.

'Not yet, Emma,' he answered, taking the small pale face between his hands, noting its tight bloodless lips. 'But we're clearing the worst section now.'

Leaving her standing behind him, helplessly waiting, he went back down once again to the pit face. As more wagons with bodies inside passed by him, his heart was very heavy. Each body in turn as it reached the surface was laid out and catalogued; ready for the family to collect.

Some were hard to identify, as fire had broken out in more places, badly burning more of the bodies. Many of them could be identified only by the numbers etched on their lamps or helmets. The atmosphere around them all was charged with the deep sorrow everyone was feeling.

Hope was fading fast now. Few injured were being brought up, mainly it was only the dead. For the men riding up in the lift with the bodies of their workmates, brothers, or even their fathers, it was a heartbreaking task.

But it was while riding up to the surface with some of these bodies that an observant rescuer noticed the fingers of one man move. Scrabbling to remove the top bodies away, he'd uncovered my nearly suffocated brother Frank, who'd been placed in the tub believed to be dead; but fortunately he was only unconscious. A few minutes more and the bodies on top of him could have taken his life too. We will, of course, always be deeply indebted to that vigilant miner.

Twenty-six men lost their lives in this tragedy. Others like my brother were lucky to escape.

Father stayed at the mine, eating and sleeping there for twelve days, until every man was accounted for, and the tunnel was made safe again. A large shadow was cast over the community for many months after.

It was eventually decided, after the investigation, that it was definitely ignited gas that had caused the explosion.

Soon after this tragedy had happened, someone came up with the idea of hanging canaries in cages down on the face. If pockets of the odourless gas then became present, the sensitive canaries would drop dead, warning the miners to get themselves out into the fresh air quickly, until the gas had dispersed itself.

My Uncle Tom bred canaries to be used down the mine.

A HARD LESSON LEARNED

Although the arrival of the pumps had brought added safety to the mines, the reservoir the mine pumped its water into was a danger in itself. Children are always fascinated by water, whether for fishing, swimming, or just floating homemade boats on. We were no exception: we were all drawn to its murky depths, even though we'd been told to keep away.

I was playing one day with my mates near the deep end of the reservoir, when one of the girls spotted a floating platform tied up close by. This was used by some of the mining engineers to plumb the water depths. The girl in question began to get too ambitious. Clambering onto the unstable platform, she began showing off by erratically jumping about on it. Despite our ignored pleas for caution, the inevitable happened, and she overbalanced and fell in.

Not being a very good swimmer, she panicked, thrashing about desperately in the water.

'Grab our hands, catch hold of our hands,' we all shouted in unison, lying on our bellies as close to the water's edge as we dared, our arms outstretched to their limits.

Frantically she lunged towards the waving hands, her strength being almost sapped. She managed at last to catch hold of one of mine and one of Gladys's hands, pulling us both into the water on top of her.

The hysterical screams of the other girls reached the ears of Mr Cox, returning home from the pumping station, who quick as a flash ran down and pulled us out. He was absolutely livid: obviously panicked by the situation, his face had turned a hue of deep purple, this profuse colour rapidly spreading down his neck before disappearing under his shirt collar.

'You bloody stupid little buggers,' he raged. 'What the hell do yer think yer playin' at? Yer could all 'ave bin drarned. Get yoursens back 'ome right now, before yer catch yer deaths of cold. And if I ever, and

I mean it, ever, catch you near this platform agen, I wunt hesitate to take me belt off to yer, all of yer. You've got no damn right to be playin' darn here anyway.'

Thank goodness we were all there together that day, or it could have been a very different story.

My second eldest sister Marion had a much worse experience of nearly drowning, when she was about twelve years of age. She was playing on her own at the time, at the corner of the reservoir where the water's pumped in from the mine. Across this corner had been placed a plank of wood, which stupidly Marion decided to hop over on one leg. Overbalancing, she fell into the water.

Marion, being a very strong swimmer, should have had no problems with this situation. But this being the place where the water came into the reservoir, she was soon being sucked under by the strong underlying currents this was creating.

Reflecting on the events at a later date, she described to me in detail what she'd experienced. How the icy chill of the water had penetrated through her clothes, completely numbing her body. She knew she wasn't in control. But she desperately fought against the whirlpool that was dragging her down into its depths; and was terrorised by it all.

She told of the feeling of light headedness that came over her, as her lungs had emptied of oxygen. Then how, suddenly, everything had changed; a feeling of peace and calmness overcoming her. She was aware of how silent and distant everything had become. A magical, almost ethereal, silence, broken spasmodically by a faint, distant tinkling sound, which had reminded her of wind chimes. And how, at this point, she had lost all her fear.

Then, just as quickly, the whole scenario changed once again. She was reluctantly jolted from this serenity by pain, searing pain. It was as if someone was ripping the scalp from her head, as the water currents pulled her one way and some unseen force pulled her the other. The pain was so intense, it caused her to momentarily pass out, before awakening to find herself lying face up in just inches of calm shallow water.

Fortunately for Marion, she hadn't been alone that day. She'd decided at the last minute to take Rover our huge Newfoundland dog along with her.

Newfoundland's are extremely strong dogs, and, like St Bernard's, were originally bred in their native country mainly for rescue work. They are especially useful in water and snow, their thick oily coats giving them insulation against the cold and wet conditions. Sensing Marion's distress, Rover's natural instincts must have kicked in, making him jump into the water looking for her, catching hold of the first thing he could find, which was a mouthful of Marion's long thick hair. He had then used his immense strength to pull her to the bank.

This whole terrifying experience must have taken just minutes from start to finish, but to Marion it had seemed like it went on forever.

A witness, who was walking his own dog around the reservoir at this time, said he couldn't believe his own eyes, at the sight of this huge dog dragging something as big as himself to the water's edge.

Rover had without a doubt saved Marion's life that day. We owed him such a lot, and were all devastated when, sadly, he had to be put to sleep at a later date.

I'll tell you more about this unfortunate event later.

THE MINERS' STRIKE

The introduction of the trade unions gave the miners a voice, causing major discontentment among those miners who were far from happy with their lot. In 1926 they decided to go out on strike, demanding better wages and working conditions; not realising at the time that the strike would last for twenty-six weeks, causing great hardship and misery for them all.

In Bermuda village, as the strike dragged on, the miners all dug up their allotments, sacrificing vegetables for the coal they found deep down underneath them. Not very much coal, but each piece they found meant warmth. And, with temperatures down to freezing at times, it took precedence over food.

They also sent out the women and children to scour the pit's waste heaps, gleaning off any small burnable bits of coal they could find, and bringing them home in old prams or on homemade handcarts. Huddled together in bed, with a glimmer of flame in the fire grate, could mean the difference between living or dying of hypothermia.

Father, being the manager, didn't agree with the strike. He tried to urge the men back to work: it was, of course, his job to do so. Deep down in his heart, though, he sympathised with their cause. He'd seen for himself the misery living on the bread line brought. He couldn't just stand by and watch them starve either.

Every Friday, towards the end of the strike, he'd have the hardest-hit families come up to the house, and would give them a shilling out of his own pocket, together with a bit of bread and cheese. Once a fortnight, in the summer months, he organised tea parties for the children on the recreation ground, providing jellies and fruit.

'Don't you get pickin' them apples in the orchard till the miners' wives have 'ad a go at 'em,' he chided us. 'Their needs, you know, are much greater than ours just now.'

He was for certain a man with compassion in his heart. Whenever I asked him if I could see down the mine, his answer was always the same: 'No! I never want yer to go darn there, wench, to see the conditions them men 'ave to work in.'

So I never did go down a mine, though most of my siblings did.

Eventually, the strike was finished, with not much achieved on either side. The management were as stubborn as the workers.

Things very gradually got back to normal again. Thin little bodies soon filled out, and rosy hues returned to white, pinched faces. A sense of euphoria filled everybody, especially the miners' wives, as once again food returned to the dinner tables.

Back at home, it was jam-making time, and we girls set about the job in hand with gusto. First, the jam jars had to be scrubbed out, then scalded in the dolly tub, before being neatly lined up on the rack above the range, to keep them warm. Then the baskets of fruit were brought in to be prepared for cooking.

Ethel, with her long pointed nails, excelled at topping and tailing the gooseberries, and also the red and blackcurrants. Mona removed all the stones from damsons, cherries, greengage and Victoria plums; while Des was roped in to peel the rhubarb and apples.

A begrudging Norman grated off the rinds of the citrus fruit ready to make the winter marmalade.

'Why is it I get all the rotten jobs, just because I'm the youngest?' I whinged at Mabel, grimacing as yet another white, wriggly body emerged from a raspberry.

'It's time you'd finished 'em and they were in the pan cookin',' she retorted back. 'An' you swat away them ruddy wasps and flies, our Marion, before they end up cooked an' all.'

Soon, everything was bubbling gently on the stove in the large brass preserving pans made for the job, the sweet, fruity aroma filling the kitchen. Marion and Mona stirred the fruit vigorously, to prevent it burning on the bottom of the pans; while mother poured that which was already cooked into the ready-warmed jam jars.

'Cut some paper circles art that greaseproof paper, Mercia, an' some string to tie 'em on with,' she shouted to me, her face flushed scarlet from the heat of the stove.

When at last all was cooked, the jars were filled with jams and marmalades of varying textures and colours. These were then lined up in their different varieties on the kitchen table to cool. Only then could the lids be tied on, the labels written and stuck on the jars.

Stacked in the pantry, these fruitful delights would wait on the shelves, to be eventually devoured, spread onto thick noggins of bread, at teatimes throughout the following year.

ANIMALS

Throughout all of my childhood we had owned many types of animals. These included horses, dogs, cats, poultry, white mice and a canary.

There was Polly the pony, who pulled our governess cart; the high trap with its two large wheels and a seat at the back. Then there was Bob the cob, who pulled the tub cart, which had side seats that faced each other, and a door at the back. These carts we had to clean and polish on Saturdays, after we had cleaned out both the stables.

Rats would come in to the stables occasionally, especially in the winter, attracted by the horses' corn feed. Father would fetch a deaf and dumb man over from nearby Griff, who owned a terrier which was a brilliant ratter. This little dog would roust the rats out into the open from under the bales of straw. Then she would leap up the walls, catching them as they tried to escape, shaking the squealing vermin from side to side in her jaws, thus preventing them from whipping round to bite her face.

We had a goat once too, which was tethered out on a long chain in the orchard. One day, Ethel decided she wanted her photo taken with our bull terrier. Both were sitting on the bench in the back garden together.

'Show us yer pearlies then, our Ethel,' said Mona, squaring up the camera ready for the big moment.

But just as she'd clicked the button, the goat had stood up on the orchard gate behind them, attracting the unwelcome attention of the dog. The bull terrier, who had never been very fond of the goat, leapt off the bench, and took off in full pursuit of it, lead still attached, with Ethel in tow. We all fell about laughing at the later developed photo, showing a horizontal Ethel and a bull terrier's backside.

But a later incident involving the bull terrier wasn't so funny. We had the canal running at the bottom of the fields, with a long brick building standing beside it. This was where the barge men, when doing long-haul trips, sometimes stabled their horses to rest overnight.

One evening, in the summertime, Dad became aware that the dog was missing from the house. Whistling and calling his name, he got no response either. Walking down the fields to look for him, his attention was caught by the sounds of men cheering and shouting, and also of dogs barking and squealing. This was all coming from the direction of the brick shed by the canal.

Alarmed and suspicious of what he was hearing, he quickly made his way in that direction. On entering the building, he was horrified by what he saw. The sight he was witnessing turned his stomach over, bringing bile to his lips. Inside were four Bermuda miners, and one of them was holding our bull terrier tightly by its collar, restricting his every movement. Meanwhile, another miner was egging on an unleashed, very vicious collie to attack him. Both dogs were already covered in each other's blood.

Not immediately seeing my father enter the building, the first miner then let loose the bull terrier, who could now defend himself against the onslaught of tearing teeth. The four men were shouting excitedly, encouraging their dog to fight, each eager to win themselves a bit of money from the wager they'd had amongst themselves, oblivious of everything but the sound of teeth on bone.

By the time father reached the far end of the long shed, where all this was taking place, it was too late; the collie was dead. Only the nerves in its body were making spasmodic, jerky movements.

Our bull terrier stood well away from it, his head drooped to the floor with exhaustion, his torn and bloodied body quivering like a jelly due to the state of shock he was in. Mortified and boiling with rage, father waded into the men, fists flying.

'I ought to rip your bloody throats out an' all, you cruel bastards,' he spluttered, hardly able to get his words out properly for the emotions he was feeling. 'Get 'ome the lot of yer. I'll sort you out tomorrow; and take that with ya.' He pointed down to the heap of flesh and fur on the floor.

Slinking out of the shed, with eyes downcast, the wary miners did as they were bid.

'It were only a bit of fun, gaffer,' one whispered softly as he passed by my father, and out into the sunshine.

When they'd gone, dad looked down at his beloved dog. The sorrowful eyes looking back at him were filled with pain. The pattern, dad knew, had now been set. After his barbaric ordeal, this dog would now savage any other dog he came in contact with, in an act of self-preservation. Maybe even a little child, if he was tormented by it. Knowing now that there was only one answer, he tied the dog up and went back to the house for his shotgun.

On returning, his heart was heavy with grief as he finished the life of his faithful friend. The next day, he called the miners into his office and sacked them all. The 'bit of fun' carried a large penalty.

I told you previously about another of our dogs, Rover, the Newfoundland who'd broken my fall when I'd fallen down the stairs on top of him. He'd also dragged Marion out of the reservoir by her hair. Obviously, we were all much indebted to him and loved him dearly.

One Sunday afternoon, mother was lying stretched on the settee in the dining room, blissfully falling into a much-needed after-dinner nap.

Suddenly, a very distressed Rover came dashing into the room and dived underneath the settee, squeaking and scratching. Now fully awake, mother was aware of the angry buzzing of insects: wasps.

Apparently, brother Des and his mates had taken the dog out walking with them, as they often did at weekends. On their travels, they had stumbled across a wasps' nest built in the hollow bottom of a decaying tree, and had stupidly got Rover to scratch it out.

Poor Rover: although the stinging eventually subsided, he reacted so badly to the wasp venom that it created a skin allergy which the vets couldn't cure him of.

This drove him demented; his constant scratching opening up sores, which soon became infected. This caused his general condition to deteriorate badly, and his quality of life became nil. One day, a gamekeeper friend of father's called in to see us, his gun tucked under his arm.

'I've come to take the dog fer a spot of rabbitin', missus,' he said to mother, calling the dog to him.

He never brought Rover back to us; and we didn't set eyes on him again after that day. Father again wept for the loss of a faithful friend, as did we all. We owed him so much; and he was such a gentle, loving dog. But Father wouldn't let him go on suffering any longer.

The smarting of Des's backside, after he'd come home on that fateful day, was nothing compared with the pain of his own conscience for years to come, because he had loved the dog just as much, if not more, than everyone else did.

It took him years to get over what had happened to Rover. He'd thought on that day that Rover would have no problems with the wasps. That the thick, long hair of the dog's coat would be a good enough barrier to stop the wasps stinging him. He hadn't reckoned with the fact that the dog could be allergic to the venom, either.

THOUGHTS OF RETIREMENT

Some of my older siblings were married by the time I was twelve years old, and at this time father was considering retiring. He'd already bought two side-by-side building plots of land, at Hilltop, in nearby Nuneaton, and plans had been drawn up to build two houses on these sites.

As the years had rolled by, he'd often sat reflecting on his life: the early years of poverty, and the struggle to keep going when his father had been killed. Also, he thought of his burning ambition for a better future, which, thank goodness, had never deserted him, and had lifted both himself and his family into a better existence. What had he achieved for others, though, he asked himself, to warrant this good fortune?

The answer to this question was that he'd done plenty.

First of all, he'd strived with others to improve the mine safety and working conditions. Also, he'd asked for a better pay deal for his workers too. All this had taken some time; but things, if not great, had improved a lot.

Secondly, he had instigated the building of the pit baths at Bermuda, where the miners could wash the thick pit dust off their bodies and hair before going home. This, he thought, had been one of the better achievements, as it not only benefited the men but the wives were grateful for this too. Now they didn't have to lug so many heavy buckets of hot water about, to fill up the tin baths. Then, there'd been the building of the Bermuda clubhouse in the village: an all-male institution that had brought a social life to the miners.

Father had, for a long time, been concerned for the safety of the village children. Before the club was built, if the men themselves weren't going out of the village for a social night in the local town pubs, then they would send out their children to buy and bring back the beer instead. This, to father, had been a dangerous practice, especially in the winter, because it was usually after dark.It was also dangerous because the children, to get to the towns, had to skirt the edges of the quarries, which were badly fenced-off, and with no proper source of lighting to shine the way. The journey had been fraught with potential hazards for these youngsters.

Now, with the building of their own village club, this had stopped this dangerous practise once and for all. He'd been glad, too, that he'd been instrumental in the laying out of the Griff and Coton cricket club. This had brought a great entertainment source to the village, boosting everyone's morale, which in itself had to be a good thing.

Lastly, and most importantly he had been liked and respected by his men. Yes, with son Frank waiting in the wings to take over from him, it would soon be time to go.

Life at the pumps was changing fast, too. Everyone was growing up and going their own ways. The latter years had been kind to the Harrison family, thanks to father. We had gradually been lifted out of a life of extreme poverty and into a life with few hardships.

I – being the youngest of the twelve children born to my mother over a long period of time, had never seen the hard times my eldest brothers and sisters had seen. For me, childhood had mostly been a wonderful experience, and I was still revelling in the innocence of it all.

My parents and my older siblings did their best to stop my bubble bursting; not in a materialistic way: we were never indulged like that. But by just trying to let childhood remain uncomplicated for myself and also the other younger brothers and sisters, for as long as possible.

Considering how much more prosperous our family had become by the time I arrived, I have never met a more grounded, down to earth, sociable bunch of people than they were; thanks to an excellent upbringing of hard work, and being taught both humility and good manners.

FRANK

Frank, my eldest brother, was nineteen years older than me, and because of this I hardly really knew him. He was very studious, just like my father, and had also started his working life as a miner on the face. He later sat for all the mining degrees, passing with flying colours; and, on father's later retirement, went on to succeed him as mine manager. But, although not disliked, Frank somehow never had the same rapport with his men as dad had; nor the respect.

Frank had one of the first motor cars in the area, a Morris Cowley, sporting an all-brass bonnet and a hood that folded down. We were all very excited when it was first delivered. It was quite a contrast from our usual pony and traps.

Later, Frank met and married a quite religious Hinckley girl named Ethel. They never did have any children of their own. I don't know whether this was intentional or unfortunate. Ethel could be a bit snobby, and more than a bit mean. When I was small, father had put a suggestion to brother Frank.

'Our Mercia will be the last babby born to yer mother an' me, our Frank. And with me being retired by the time she grows up to a marriageable age, money won't be available for her, as it was fer you. You and me, we both 'ave got good jobs now. So how abart we put a shillin' a week into a bank account for her, till she's twenty-one?' Frank agreed that it was a good idea: so, every week, this is what they did. Three months later, though, just after his marriage to Ethel, Frank's generosity stopped. From then on, every penny Frank earned would be going into Ethel's purse, and no one else's; she'd see to that. Father was miffed for a while that Frank hadn't stood up to her a bit more.

My eldest niece, Marion's daughter Christine, herself now in her eighties, recently told us her childhood memories of Ethel's stinginess.

'As you know,' she recalled, 'we were living in one of the little pit houses in Bermuda village, my father also being a miner. Like most of the other mining families living there, we were quite poor at the time.

One of the highlights for me was when Grandad Harrison would come flying through the village in his pony and trap on his way to the mine. If I heard him coming, I would run out and swing on the garden gate to wave to him. And when he saw me, he'd throw me three pence for some sweets.

Also, another highlight for us was when we were taken up to the big house "The Pumps". Grandad would play all sorts of games with myself, my siblings, and some of my cousins.

Emptying his pockets when he came in, he would throw us pennies from over the upstairs balcony, which clattered and rolled as they fell down onto the tiled floor below. We children would be waiting excitedly downstairs to scrabble for them. Alternatively, he would hide them around the house for us to find.

It was on these occasions that, if Uncle Frank's Ethel was around, the full extent of her lack of pride when it came to money came to the fore. Dressed in all her finery, she'd think nothing of scrabbling on the floor with us, pushing us aside to pick up the pennies first, and pocketing as many as she could. It's always stuck in my mind how someone with a much grander lifestyle could deprive us of the pennies that meant so much to us. I'm surprised really that Grandad didn't say something to her. But perhaps he didn't want to stir up trouble for Uncle Frank.'

'Also,' Christine continued, 'after Grandad had retired, and Uncle Frank and Ethel moved into "The Pumps", whenever I asked mother if I could go up to the big house for some apples from the orchard, she would insist that I take tuppence with me to pay for them. And Aunt Ethel would always take the money off me.

The only time I was deemed fit to sit at Aunt Ethel's table was when I passed a scholarship to attend the local high school, which was no mean feat in those days, considering our, at that time, deprived lifestyle. A message had come from the big house, saying Christine could come for tea. Needless to say, I politely declined the offer.

I didn't get to the high school either, as my mother and father couldn't afford the required school uniform. They were too proud to let Grandad and Grandma buy it for me, even though they offered.'

Although now a wealthy man, after Frank's death, not a penny of his money was left to any member of his own family or friends. Ethel, with no children of her own to consider, willed it all to her own side of the family when she passed away a few years later.

Mabel's wedding.

MABEL

Getting back to the lives of my siblings, Marion was the next one after Frank to get married. It was to be quite a rushed, no frills affair. Marion, being strong willed and very impulsive, didn't want to wait. Also, the union not being altogether approved of by father, didn't help her cause either. But more about this later.

Next to leave home was Mabel, my beloved surrogate mother. She'd always been there for me in my life. Often as a disciplinarian tyrant, but also as a second mother, picking up the pieces after any crisis in my young life. Made to stay at home to help mother, she'd had a hard life. She was the eldest and definitely the prettiest of the girls. Her social life, though, had been very limited due to mother's ever-expanding brood.

Mabel, being the second eldest child, had experienced much of the poverty of the earlier days. No such thing as a doll in Mabel's Christmas stocking. Her present was always an apron, which every year got a bit fancier. As she got older, she had to take on more and more responsibility of the household.

A washer-woman now helped with the laundry. But it was Mabel's job to get the copper filled and boiling, ready for the washing of the linen. This was followed on by all the boys' dirty pit clothes, which she'd have to help scrub.She also had to be up at 4 am to light the fires; also to cut and pack the boys' and father's pit meals; then be ready and available to get breakfast for five o'clock.

Her labour of love, though, was the flower garden, which relaxed her. She dug a garden as well, if not better, than any man could. Helped by my mother, she produced different blooms, of every colour imaginable. The garden was always kept immaculately tidy with not a weed in sight.

As some of the other girls grew up and started work, Mabel tried to rebel a bit by going for a job at the nearby Lister's velvet factory. Because she was such a superb needle-woman, she easily got the job.

But father objected strongly, saying there was plenty of work for her to do at home. He did, however, let her go to a cookery school, and this made her a brilliant cook. She was also given complete control of we younger children, and she'd stand no nonsense.

If we ever came home from school with a few lodgers in our hair, it was Mabel's job to get rid of them, and she was none too gentle.

'Dirty little sods,' she'd say, scrubbing our scalps till they were raw; giving us a good slap if we pulled away.

Once Des and I had whooping cough, and were off school. We were making a general nuisance of ourselves by whining and attention seeking. Mabel, trying hard to catch up on her chores, was busy black-leading the fire grate, and Des stood nearby, coughing all over her. At last losing her patience, she threw the blacking brushes to the floor.

'Right, that's it! I've just abart had enough of you two splutterin' all over me,' she shouted venomously. 'Sit darn over there, an' don't you move.'

Reaching into the top kitchen cupboard, she produced a bottle of black liquid, which she shook vigorously.

'I ain't 'avin' you two barkin' over me all day,' she hissed. 'When I've given you two a dose of this stuff it'll soon quieten yer darn for a while, that's fer sure.'

She spooned a good dose of the foul-tasting liquid down our throats, then went back to her black-leading. But she had hardly started again before Des and I became violently sick, all over the floor.

'Bloody hell, look at me floor,' she raged. 'An' I've just scrubbed it. Get out into the fresh air, both of yer,' she shouted, waving her arms about like something demented.

Needing no prompting, we ran straight outside and into the arms of Granny Mockford the midwife, who was on a social call to see mother.

'What the heck's goin' on 'ere? What's the matter wi' these kids, Mabel?' she enquired sternly. 'They're sickin' their innards up out 'ere and they look awful.'

'Nothin' at all's wrong wi' 'em,' Mabel replied sheepishly. 'I've just doped 'em up a bit to stop 'em coughin', but I think I've given 'em too much.'

Not at all amused by Mabel's last statement, granny retaliated angrily.

'You wanna be a bit more tolerant, Mabel 'Arrison. You could have killed the poor little buggers,' she reprimanded.

But I have to admit: though Mabel was a bit stupid, doing what she did, she did stop us coughing, because we slept most of the day afterwards.

Although it was a justified tongue lashing Mabel got that day, I could understand why she had such a short fuse at times, because she had some rotten jobs to do. I remember another time, when I was quite young, seeing her scrubbing away in the scullery sink on what looked like bits of rag.

'What you doin' that for?' I asked of her, curiously. 'What's them bits of rag for, an' why's there blood on 'em; where's it come from?'

Harassed and weary of my continuous chatter, Mabel replied tartly.

'There's blood on 'em cos I've just cut me bloody throat. An' if you keep on as you'r doin', I'll probably cut your's an' all.'

When I grew up I realised the rags were sanitary wear for the older girls. No such thing as sanitary towels in those days. So, as always, poor Mabel had the job of scrubbing and boiling the bits of cloth. She was made to take over the mother role when she was only a girl herself. But, despite her many frustrations, she loved all her brothers and sisters very much.

Although strict, she was always on hand to soothe a wounded knee or wipe away a tear.

Now, though, our lives were going to change: Mabel was getting married. The lucky man in question was Herbert Sharratt, a tall, gentle giant of a man, who played rugby for Leicester Tigers. Marrying Mabel, he would have everything a man could wish for. She was pretty, domesticated, excellent mother potential, and was a very accomplished seamstress.

Mabel's sewing and crocheting were superb, and had won her a prize from the *Daily Mail* newspaper.

This was awarded to her for a tablecloth she'd once crocheted. The corners of this cloth were very deep, and on each one were spider webs and hanging roses, each petal lifting up individually. It was a really beautiful piece of work and deserved to win the first prize.

When the First World War was on, she embroidered two samplers. These mother had framed and hung up on the parlour wall. One featured a Union Jack flag, lying in intricate folds. And on top of this sat a British bulldog which held a smaller Union Jack in its mouth.

Underneath this first scene, she had embroidered the words 'United We Stand'.

The other sampler had the bulldog standing over a ripped-up Union Jack flag, and embroidered underneath this one were the words 'Divided We Fall'. Her intricate stitching ensured the quality of her embroidery was always superb.

Later, she crocheted a deep edging for another table cloth, but this she never got round to finishing. After doing three sides, it was wrapped in tissue paper and shoved in a draw. There it remained until she died, aged eighty-seven. It was then given to my sister Ethel, who in later years passed it on to me.

I donated it to Barwell church in Leicestershire, the village where I now live. Here, a clever parishioner finished the lace, then used it to edge an altar cloth, where it remains to this day. It has to be over a hundred years old now, at least.

Mabel's wedding was to be a grand affair: we girls were all bridesmaids, and father stumping up to give her the best he could afford; a fitting reward for all her years of hard work. A marquee was erected in the garden for the reception, and her wedding dress came from Paris; an almost unheard-of thing for the working class in those days.

The only thing he wouldn't give her was his arm to the altar. 'I'll never give my daughters away to anyone,' he vowed, and never did. Not one of his girls did he give away. If he'd had his own way, he would have kept all his children at home for ever. He loved his family environment so much, and didn't ever want it to break up. But he must have known that, in reality, this could never be.

The happy couple went to live in Hinckley, where she gave birth to her only child, a son she called Herbert, named after his father. Life must have been much easier for her now she hadn't got all us children to look after; though she must have missed us being constantly around her for a while.

I still laugh to myself when I recall the memory of mother, Mabel, myself and young Herbert going into a shop to buy hen food. There were quite a lot of people in front of us in the queue, waiting to be served; and, as we stood in line, Herbert's attention was drawn to a cage of white mice that stood on a table at the side of his pram. All of a sudden, he started to shout excitedly and very loud.

'Look there, our mam, that mouse, it's just 'ad a wee! Where did it come from, art its mouff, or art its arse?'

We didn't know where to put ourselves: mother was in stitches. She had to cross her legs to stop from wetting herself. Mabel, red with embarrassment, put her hand over his mouth to shut him up. What a good laugh we all had on our way back.

When Mabel grew older, she was very interested in the spiritualist church, and became a staunch member. When she left home after her marriage, I missed her dreadfully. The house was never the same again to me. Ethel had to stay at home for a while to look after us.

Sadly, young Herbert, when grown up and married himself, died suddenly at his home. It was a terrible shock to his wife Lily, and his young daughter Lisa. Mabel felt it terribly too: it must be an awful thing for any parent, when a child dies before they do. Especially an only child. The rest of the family were gutted too; he was such a jolly person.

Mabel, lived to be eighty-seven: Her funeral, held at the spiritual church, was the most uplifting service I've ever attended.

Ethel was training to be a milliner at the time Mabel got married. The hats she made were beautiful. It was a shame she had to give up her career to look after us. It would have been Marion who stayed at home next, as she was the second eldest girl. But she was already married herself and had opted to work in the munitions factory, doing her bit, as she put it, towards the war effort, which was just beginning.

THE PREDICTION

Marion was a different kettle of fish altogether from Mabel's more sensible approach to life. She was always great fun, outgoing, bubbly, kind, generous, and easy going, with a brilliant sense of humour, which often got her into mischief. But she could also be strong willed, a bit wayward, stubborn, even rebellious at times, if she felt justified.

Both she and the next born, Jack, were of the same temperament, though Jack was not rebellious. They were inseparable, double trouble, you might say, and they kept everyone alive with their antics.

From the age of ten, Marion often went to stay with one of father's sisters, Betsy, who, together with her husband Jack Sharratt, ran the Anchor pub at the bottom of Old Roadway, Bedworth. Betsy, who had no children of her own, was very fond of Marion; and, finding it nice to be doted on, Marion willingly commuted from one home to another as she grew up.

One of Marion's best friends was a Bedworth girl named Sarah. She lived with her doting family, including granny, who was well known in the town as a spiritualist medium. Sarah was out playing hopscotch with Marion one day when someone from the town approached her.

'You 'ave to come 'ome with me at once, gel,' he said to Sarah. 'Cos yer granny's dyin' an' she's askin' for you.'

Sarah was absolutely mortified at this news, as she absolutely idolised her granny.

'I ain't goin' without you come with me, Marion,' she blubbered tearfully, clutching her best friend's hand tightly.

Both walked back to the little terraced house together and climbed up the stairs to see granny. Lying in her bed, surrounded by her family, the old lady lay silent and still. Suddenly, granny's heavily wrinkled eyelids flew open, and her pale, watery eyes struggled to focus.

Instinctively, she must have known that Sarah was now in the room.

Turning her head towards the door, she signalled weakly with a long, bony finger, for her granddaughter to come closer to her. Bending down, Sarah rested her face against her beloved granny's wizened cheeks, trying to catch her words.

'I waited for you, Sarah,' granny rasped hoarsely, grasping on to Sarah's jumper. 'I couldn't go to me maker yet, afore telling yer that I'm passin' all me powers on to you. But listen to me carefully now: just make sure you use 'em wisely.'

Marion listened to them, silently spellbound, but the conversation was short, granny slipping away quietly to a better world, with everyone around the bedside weeping for the loss of her.

When she grew up, Sarah married a man named Poutney, and went to live with him at Mill Farm, Griff. This was the farm George Eliot immortalised in her novel, *The Mill on the Floss*. After her marriage, Sarah became a recluse, rarely leaving the farm; hardly anyone saw her, including Marion. Local folk said she'd become quite weird, wearing long skirts that came down to the floor, with a man's trilby always on her head.

One sunny day, Marion said to Mona and myself:

'Let's go for a picnic over on the Arbury estate and see if we can find Sarah Poutney. I 'aven't seen hair nor hide of her fer years.'

Eager to do something different for a change, off we all went, trudging across the many fields that would take us to Arbury, passing the huge gates into Arbury Hall, before crossing on to the lane that led to Mill Farm. As we turned a corner and approached the farm, we were more than surprised to see Sarah herself leaning over the yard gate.

'Hello there, Marie,' she said to Marion. 'I've bin waitin' for you to arrive. I knew yer were comin', so I've put the kettle on for a cuppa.'

We were flabbergasted; but, ignoring mine and Mona's look of total disbelief, Sarah hugged Marion tightly.

'It's great to see you again, Marie, after all this time. We 'ave such a lot of news ter catch up on,' she said happily. 'Come into the field and let me find you somewhere nice to have your picnic.'

She took us into a shady clearing, between some trees. I was quick to notice a dead tree lying in the grass, and pointed it out to the girls.

'That'll make a good picnic table for us, that old log over there,' I said.

So we sorted ourselves out while Sarah went to fetch the tea.

On her return, Sarah took off her trilby and sat down, talking to Marion, then turned herself around to face me.

'So, Mercia, you think this is just an old log do yer? Well, yer shouldn't allas tek things at face value. Things ain't always as they seem ter be, you know.'

She continued on, placing the old trilby back on her head, shading the sun from her eyes, 'See them two trees over there behind yer? One leanin' itsen on the other.'

I looked back behind me, noting a tall straight tree with a smaller one leaning into it.

'Well, that larger tree is the king, the other one's his queen. She's in sorrow; he's got his arms around her, comforting her. Can you see the jewels sparkling in their crowns?'

She pointed her fingers upwards to the sunlight shining through the branches.

'This log that your sittin' on is their son: there was a terrible storm, and he was killed.'

Then, turning herself back to Marion, she continued with her chat.

Leaning over discreetly towards Mona, I whispered in her ear. 'Blimey, she is weird, isn't she, and how did she know we were comin'? We haven't seen her in years.'

Our previous conversation was soon forgotten, as we ate our food and prattled on about anything and everything. Sarah, who was still catching up on all the local news, then turned to me again.

'Your goin' out wi' a fair-haired lad, ain't yer, Mercia,' she said, dropping her head down on to her chest thoughtfully.

Oh lord, I thought, now I'm in for it. I hope Mona doesn't tell me mam.

'He's a nice enough lad,' Sarah mused, 'but it won't last.' She then went quiet for a moment before finally adding: 'I can see miles and miles of sand, pyramids, and camels. Standing beside these camels is a man with very dark skin and black hair. One day you'll meet up wi' this fella: it'll be like puttin' a needle to a magnet. An' nothing will ever part yer, only death.'

After we'd finished our picnic, we went for a walk in the fields alongside the mill stream. Every now and again Sarah would spot something in the water, a leaf, a flower head or a twig. She'd bend down, plucking them from the silvery ripples; chanting beautiful poetry to herself. The hem of her skirt dipped in the water as she walked.

'Do you think you'll always stay here, Sarah?' enquired Mona, trying to make some conversation.

'Yes, I suppose I will,' Sarah replied despondently. 'Although I get a bit fed up at times cos I don't see many people.

Sir Francis Newdigate, the owner of the Arbury estate, he sends 'is friends up 'ere sometimes ter see me. But I ain't daft: I know why they come. I tell 'em now't of interest to 'em. I reserve my gift.'

On the way home, leaving a forlorn Sarah waving from the gate, we laughed about the events of the day.

'Can't wait to meet my dark-haired Arab,' I giggled gaily, little knowing that a few years later, while attending a party, I was to meet my future husband.

Ten years older than me, he was a long-serving soldier in the army. He'd just returned with his regiment to England, after spending several years stationed in Egypt. His skin was darkly tanned, under a head of black hair. And nothing but his death parted us.

Sarah's predictions frightened many people. Behind her back, they called her a witch.

Eric Olner, a local lad, regularly used to bike over to the farm next to Sarah's to see his friends, Jim the local milkman and his wife Lizzie. One night, after a late game of cards, Eric picked up his coat from the back of his chair and made ready to leave.

'Blimey, it's twelve o'clock already, time I'd long gone,' he said tiredly, thanking them both for their hospitality.

Retrieving his bike from the dairy wall, Eric set off, thinking to himself what a lovely moonlight night it was, as he pedalled his bike lazily through Arbury woods, heading for his home. Suddenly, out of the corner of his eye, he spotted some movement in the trees at the side of him.

'What was that?' he spoke out loudly to himself. 'Was that a deer or was it a fox?'

But when he came to the next clearing, he was faced with what looked like a ghostly apparition: it was Sarah. Dressed in a long, almost opaque white nightdress, she ran in and out of the trees; her arms outstretched, the moonlight reflecting on her lithe, supple body, giving an almost iridescent glow to her flowing form.

The petrified Eric, thinking he was actually seeing a ghost, pedalled his bike as fast as his legs could take him, never stopping until he'd reached the safety of his house. Recalling these events to me at a later date, he said to me soberly: 'Mercia, I aint ashamed to say it to yer. But I shit myself that night.'

It seems, from what other people have said, Sarah often ran in the woods late at night.

'I like to be as one with the animals,' she had said. 'They are my true friends, they never lie to me. We have an understanding. A mutual trust of each other. They have no fear of me at all.'

MARION

As I said earlier, Marion was a lovely person; full of fun, with a natural wit that rolled off her tongue spontaneously. She had also been blessed with the most beautiful head of reddish brown hair, which was long, thick and a mass of natural waves; different to the rest of the girls in the family, as we all had fine, silkier hair.

Marion would never wash her hair in anything but rain water. She rarely used tap water, preferring to dip her head into the rain water butt that stood beside the kitchen door under the spouting. Because of this, her hair was always shiny and healthy looking. A downside was that, because of its wiry texture, she always had difficulty keeping those springy waves under the control of any pins or combs. Both Marion and brother Jack were always very close to each other. Having the same outrageous sense of humour ensured that the occupants of our house were never dull for very long.

One winter's night, when Marion was about nine years old, we girls were as usual in the bedroom together, sleeping off what had been another hard day at school. Marion, who didn't feel at all tired at this stage, pulled the lighted candle closer to the edge of the bedside table, trying to cast more light onto the book she was currently reading.

Completely engrossed in what was a nail-biting story, she fought off the drowsiness that was beginning to envelope her. Her eyelids were becoming increasingly heavy at this point. Eventually, though, tiredness overcame her, and she fell asleep with the book still in her hand.

I don't know how long she'd been sleeping before the strong smell of singed hair filled her nostrils, bringing her deep slumber to an abrupt end. But it had been enough time for the flame of the candle to set light to the edge of her pillow and smoulder its way along the side of her bed towards her feet.

Screaming in terror, Marion soon had everyone in the house awake, and we were all evacuated into the garden, leaving father and a couple of the older boys to run up the stairs with buckets of water to extinguish the fire. We were lucky that Marion had woken up. The whole of the house could have gone up in flames if she hadn't have done so. It just shows how easily these things can happen: obviously she must have forgotten to blow out the precariously placed candle, and had knocked it off the table onto the bed while asleep. Thinking about it, there must have been numerous cases of families being burnt to death due to candles in that era.

As I told you earlier: Marion spent much of her time as a child and young adult with our Auntie Betsy, father's sister, who, together with her husband, kept a public house in nearby Bedworth town. And it was while working at Aunt Betsy's pub that Marion met her future husband, Chris Cole. A young Bedworth soldier home on leave, Chris was both charming and flattering, soon having Marion completely besotted with him.

Knowing the relationship would never be tolerated by father because of her young age, Marion regularly had clandestine meetings with Chris at night, under the cover of darkness, aided and abetted by brother Jack. Father eventually caught her out though, and she was grounded for a while, which didn't please her.

By being kept away from Chris, Marion's rebellious streak had now surfaced big time; and she made it quite clear to everyone involved, including father, that, whatever obstacles were put in front of her, she was going to marry Chris. She even threatened to elope with him if the need arose.

After leaving the army for good, Chris asked father properly if he could marry Marion. But father, through either intuition or sheer stubbornness, was still unsure about the union. Eventually, on Marion's continual insistence, he reluctantly gave in and agreed to the marriage. He also gave Chris a job down the mine, at the same time lecturing him on the fact that Marion had been looked after all her life, and that he expected Chris to do the same.

After a quick no-frills wedding – because Marion wouldn't wait for a proper one to be organised for her – the happy couple moved into a little Bedworth terrace, together with Chris's mother. For the first months of marriage everything seemed to be going really well for them both. But for the next four years life was to be far from a bed of roses for Marion.

Like many men do, Chris was finding it really difficult to adjust to life outside the army. Three children had been born to them quite quickly, and Mrs Cole senior was also at that time giving Marion a rough ride. As if this wasn't enough, Chris started drinking heavily, missing his shifts at the mine more and more. Consequently, money was now getting tight, so food rations were becoming less.

Even so, Chris still expected his large dinners to be on the table every night. Rather than cause aggravation, and risk the wrath of Chris's Mother, Marion took to skipping meals, giving most of her share to the children. When she visited us at home, it soon became apparent how much weight she had lost, her dresses now hanging loosely on a once well-covered frame. She was also losing much of the effervescent sparkle she'd always had, too. It was also inevitable that my father would be told by his overseers how Chris was often bunking off work; and how, when he did turn up, he didn't pull his weight, being constantly hung over from the previous night's drinking.

Father was livid: after hauling Chris into his office, he gave him the works.

'Just because you're me son-in-law,' he ranted, 'don't give you privileges over anyone else. Anybody who don't pull his weight darn this pit faces the same consequences, and, as in your case, deserves the bloody sack. You've neglected me daughter; she's goin' darn to skin and bone. And I'll tell yer this, I've begged 'er to come home, and I know in her 'eart she wants to. But she's loyal, is our Marion, big 'earted as they come. Different from the idle bastard she's married to. So, from today, I'm putting you on a job where you've got ter work harder for yer money. I'm also givin' you one of the empty Bermuda pit houses, so that Marion can get away from that old harridan of a mother of yours; which should give her some peace of mind, if that's possible livin' with a bugger like you. Now get out me sight, cos you won't get another chance, believe me.'

For quite a time after they'd moved to Bermuda village, things were much better for the Cole family. But, unfortunately, Chris still couldn't cope with the responsibilities attached to life in the outside world, after the close comradeship and the security of his army life, which had cocooned him from the harsh realities that life in the real world could inflict on a man in this era. So he continued to block everything out with the only thing that gave him confidence: alcohol.

Eventually, the pull of the new club house in the village became too much of a temptation too, and things slipped back once again to how they were before. After his shift, when he bothered to go, Chris went straight into the club, drinking himself silly, before he went home for his dinner. Mother often sent me over to Bermuda with food for them all. It was obvious Marion still wasn't having enough to eat; it showed in her pale, pinched face.

I wanted so much to bring both her and the three babies back home with me, to make things right for her. It wasn't that Chris was a bad person at all; in fact, he was just the opposite: quite an affable person really. He was not bad tempered, and never violent, even in drink. Just, at this time in his life, confused, weak willed, and lazy.

We were all aware that he thought the world of Marion, so it must have given his conscience a twinge to cause her so much worry and stress. But he was out of control with his drinking now, and couldn't get a grip on himself.

Seeing her children having less food than she thought they should started to bring out an aggression in Marion that belied her usual sunny nature. She was almost at breaking point, sliding into a depression when Chris came home with half a wage; the rest, as she put it, he'd pissed up the wall.

The very last time I took food over to Bermuda, Marion confided in me. Chris had gone to the club as usual, and she was trying to make a meal out of various bits and bobs she'd found in the pantry. Clearly depressed, but pleased to have someone close to confide in, she let out to me all her suppressed feelings.

'I've nearly reached the end of me tether now, our Mercia, I'm at me wits end. The kids seem to be allas hungry, an' forever got snotty noses. He don't give a damn, just laughs everythin' off, thinks just of his sen. He ain't worked for four days this week, but he's bin darn to the club every day. I daren't even think of tellin' me dad, cos he'd kill him.

Trying to cheer her up, I changed the subject, chatting about all the things that had happened at home recently. Later, after the children were put to bed, Marion and I huddled together on the threadbare sofa, enjoying the warmth of the fire on our faces from the open door of the range, even having a bit of a laugh about this and that. While, poised above our heads, Chris's dinner sat spoiling on the rack.

The sudden lifting up of the door latch signified Chris's arrival, and I saw Marion visibly tense up as he entered the room, clearly the worst for drink. A huge big grin spread quickly over his face at the sight of us both.

'Hello there, Mercia,' he greeted me warmly, then leant over towards Marion.

'An 'ow's me beautiful little Marie then?' he slurred, winking at her cheekily, before sitting down at the table.

'I 'ope you've got me dinner ready, an' plenty of it, me gel, cos I'm bloody starvin'.'

He playfully banged the table with his fork as he spoke.

Marion was furious, but mostly embarrassed that I was here witnessing his drunken behaviour. Before common sense could prevail, her pent-up feelings finally boiled over. She flew to the table, picking up the first thing that came to hand.

'You'll get what's comin' to yer all right,' she spat at him through tight lips. 'But it ain't your dinner. This is something you won't want.'

And with these words said, she threw with all her strength the object she had in her hand.

Chris quickly saw it coming, and reeled backwards unsteadily, holding his hands up in horror. The pointed blade of the knife found its target, going right through the fleshy part of his palm, pinning his hand to the pantry door.

I just sat there staring. I was totally dumbstruck.

'Marion! What have you done?' I exclaimed, once my faculties had returned.

'It should've bin his bloody throat,' was all she could mutter dejectedly, clearly beyond any feelings of remorse at this stage.

Luckily, the knife had gone through cleanly, missing all the major nerves and larger blood vessels.

The mental effect, though, that this whole scenario had on Chris was amazing. It was just as if the shock of it all had brought him to his senses. He never again drunk heavily, or tried to shirk off work. Father gave him his old job back, and he became a loving, attentive husband and father once again. And, happily for everyone concerned, he never once slipped back again.

Marion bloomed once more: back came her lovely rosy cheeks, and most importantly her wonderful sense of humour. Everyone in the village was pleased to see them both back to their old cheerful selves again, Marion's quick humour once more brightening many a dismal day. Marion loved all the village children too, and would regularly take in, as she called it, 'a raggedy-arsed kid'; then sit at her sewing machine and run him up a pair of trousers from pieces of old material. Life for them was good again, and they lived a very happy life together with their three children, Tom, Christine, and Brian.

JACK

Brother Jack was the next one to leave home. He was now an electrician at Measham pit in Leicestershire. It was here at Measham that he met and married his wife, Dolly. Always the joker, his antics brought hours of laughter into our home as he grew up. Cheeky and cheerful, he and Marion had been the perfect foil for one another, each one egging the other on. Never a dull moment when they were together.

At the 'Pumps' the boys all slept together in the same room, the window opening above a sloping veranda roof.

When Marion started seeing Chris, and everyone else in the house was asleep, Jack would lower her down on to this roof, then, sliding to the ground, she'd go off for a 'rendezvous' with Chris. Throwing pebbles at the window on her return, Jack would haul her back up into the house again.

Eventually, though, she'd come unstuck when father had caught her out. He had given her a good hiding, and banned her from seeing Chris in the foreseeable future.The very next evening, after a quiet discussion with Jack, Marion disappeared from the house, and didn't come back all night. Finding her still made-up bed empty, early the next morning, the family were going frantic. As soon as they were able, as the dawn turned to daylight, Dad and the boys, together with some of the local miners, searched the surrounding fields and woods.

But they found nothing. It was only when Dad said he was calling in the police that Jack had to own up. He confessed to everyone involved in the search that Marion, still sulking from being grounded, was hiding behind a stack of plant pots, under the greenhouse staging; and that he'd aided and abetted her by smuggling out food for her at breakfast. Needless to say, from an extremely angry, stressed, and also embarrassed father, they both learnt a hard lesson that day

Another escapade happened one evening after we younger ones had been sent early to bed.

We were all woken up by the sound of Mabel screaming loudly downstairs. Running out on to the landing, and looking over the balcony, we saw the door of the glory hole (the cupboard under the stairs) open. Out came Jack with a very limp Mabel hanging over his shoulder. A rivulet of red liquid was trickling from the side of her mouth, which was emphasised by the chalky whiteness of her face.

Seeing our startled faces, Jack explained to us how he'd just murdered Mabel after a squabble, and was just about to bury her in the garden. We screamed and cried so much at this news, it caused Jack to fall to his knees in mirth, dropping Mabel in the process. She, to our astonishment, jumped up, grinning broadly from ear to ear, wiping off some of the thick make-up she'd plastered on her face, onto her cardigan sleeve, and howling with laughter at the sight of our distraught faces. We children were not at all amused though, and let them both know so, in no uncertain terms.

It seems that, because mother and father were both out for the evening, they'd decided to help themselves to the home-made elderberry wine, and were both quite merry. The effects of the alcohol had triggered off the evening's chain of events.

Winding us up was just another example of the numerous charades that Jack's wicked sense of humour brought to the household.

When Jack was about five years old, he was at home when the doctor called socially to see my father. On entering the front parlour, the doctor didn't immediately see the cat lying just to the side of the doorway, and he accidentally trod on its tail. This caused the offended animal to spit and squeal, before twisting round and sinking its claws and teeth into the soft flesh of the doctor's lower leg.

'Damn and blast that animal,' he exclaimed angrily, trying to extricate himself from the viciously sharp talons.

'That's the second time lately that I've been savaged by that damn thing.'

He rubbed his hand over the small but deep puncture wounds, smearing the thin rivulets of blood as he did so.

'I'd give five pounds to anyone who'd cut the tail off that bloody cat. Then I wouldn't be treading on the damn thing again,' he mumbled grumpily, before sitting down to a hot cup of tea, laced with a generous measure of father's whisky; this accompanied by a large slice of mother's fruit and ale cake.

A pleasant hour was spent by all, as everyone was brought up to date with all the latest news and gossip.

'Time I was on my way now,' said the doctor, picking up his coat. 'Thanks for your hospitality, folks, and the cake, Emma, it was as usual delicious.'

Then, after saying his goodbyes to everyone, he left the house.

On leaving by the back door, the doctor strolled leisurely up the side path, before turning round the corner of the house and on to the front drive. Suddenly, his attention was caught by a sharp 'psst, psst' coming from behind the garden trellis. Turning around, he saw Jack beckoning to him, with a big wide grin on his face.

'Well, what is it, Jack? What can I be doing for you, m'lad?' the doctor enquired curiously.

'You can gimme the fiver yer promised, doc,' replied Jack, who was flushed with excitement. 'Cos I've just done what you asked for: the bloody cat won't give you any more trouble now.'

Bending down into a box at his feet, Jack brought out a very miserable feline, which now looked more like a Manx cat, as its once beautiful fluffy tail was now only a stump.

Seeing the look of horror on the doctor's face, Jack ran over and patted his arm consolingly.

'Now, don't you go looking so worried, doc,' he explained innocently.

'I didn't actually cut it off, you know; I shut it in the greenhouse door instead, cos it was quicker and less painful.'

Needless to say, Jack didn't get his fiver, and we won't go into what he did get. The poor doctor, however, felt a pang of guilt every time he set eyes on the cat. Putting a few stitches in the end of its stump had led to a quick recovery. But he always felt he must be the cat's number one enemy, since that fateful day. He also vowed to watch what he said in the presence of young children in the future. The whole thing was a talking point in our house for years, and still is.

At this point, you the readers probably think my parents were rearing a budding psychopath. But, fortunately, this was not so. This cruel event was a one-off situation, and Jack, thank goodness, grew up a kind and caring person. Even he must have cringed at the terrible thing he had done, when he was old enough to realise the enormity of it.

Jack, when he started work, used to be on a regular night shift at the pit. Since the older girls had got married, it was his job when he returned home in the mornings to get we younger ones up for school, and give us our breakfasts. He would make sure we all washed properly, feed us, then give us all a nice hot cup of tea.

Breakfast time with Jack was usually great, because he made us laugh so much. But every now and then he would wipe the smiles off our faces by lacing the teapot with Epsom salts. He would then stand back to witness the grimaces that appeared on our faces, trying hard not to laugh at our discomfort. Always making sure we drank every drop of it.

'Get it darn yer necks,' he'd instruct us firmly. 'It'll clean yer innards out.'

I would cry sometimes, because it tasted so horrible. Jack never relented though.

'It'll 'elp keep you well,' he would say.

Maybe there was some truth in this statement, as we were rarely ill.

One night, when we were a bit younger, we girls were in our bedroom, all getting ready for bed. Suddenly, a loud thumping on the adjoining door that separated our bedroom at the front of the house from the boys' bedroom at the back, caught our attention. Always kept locked, Jack's voice was muffled as he leant against it.

'Marion! Marion! Can you hear me in there,' he shouted loudly.

'I've got sommat really interestin' I want ter tell yer.'

Marion got out of bed, eager for a bit of gossip, and went over to the door. Pressing her head hard against it, she tapped it lightly, letting Jack know she was there.

Jack's voice, now hardly discernible, was coming back through to her.

'I can't hear yer, Jack,' she shouted out loudly to him. 'You'll have ter speak up a bit more.'

'Put yer ear by the keyhole, then you'll hear me better,' Jack replied. 'I can't shout any louder, the other lads are sleepin' now.'

We girls watched, intrigued, as Marion dropped to her knees by the door, then pressed her ear to the keyhole.

'Come on then, Jack, give it to me, I can hear yer now.'

This statement from Marion was quickly followed by a loud scream, as she pulled sharply away from the door, a look of sheer horror transforming her face.

'The dirty bugger's just piddled in me ear through the bloody keyhole,' she gasped.

The raucous laughter of the other lads next door did nothing to soothe Marion's ruffled feathers. We girls discreetly hid our faces under the bedclothes, trying to suppress our giggles.

Jack eventually met and married his Dolly, a girl who worked in the offices at the Measham colliery, where he was eventually made up to chief electrician. They lived in Measham all their lives after they married, and had one son, Frankie.

I don't think I ever met a funnier, more laid back man than Jack was. And his dry sense of humour, antics, and practical jokes were badly missed by all of us still left at home. Dolly was a good sort. She was the ideal match for him, as she had a great sense of humour too.

FATHER'S RETIREMENT

In 1927 father finally retired, and his eldest son Frank succeeded him as mine manager. Although the mine owners had told him he could stay in the big house, father said no.

'That house was meant for the pit manager. I know the young uns will be gutted ter move out, but it's only fair our Frank should 'ave it,' he said. So, temporarily, we had to move into Frank and Ethel's cramped little terraced house in Nuneaton town, while our new house at Hilltop was being finished. I hated every moment of it: missing the fresh air and freedom we had at the old house, its beautiful surroundings, and the nearness of my friends.

There I had left behind my childhood, the cherished memories, moments that could never come back, but that I'd never forget. The old house was the place in which I'd experienced a youth that some could only have dreamed of.

Eventually, our new house was finished, and I have to say it was a fine one. Though much smaller than the 'Pumps', it was still quite spacious, with a lovely oak staircase, and had several beautiful stained-glass windows. The back garden was reasonably large, though narrower and very long, its boundary at the bottom being skirted once again by the canal. And it was here that my father, mother, and we siblings that were still at home settled into a quieter, but happy existence.

When he'd finished working at the mine, the colliery bosses had presented dad with a beautiful gold pocket watch. It was inscribed with his name, Francis Harrison, inside its lid; also with recognition and thanks for the service he'd given to the company. The watch was attached to a thick gold chain, with a guard in the shape of a shield on the other end. He carried the watch in his waistcoat pocket, with the chain draped across his chest, the guard fastening into one of his buttonholes, which was the fashion of the day.

Although my father's eyesight was deteriorating quite badly these days, it didn't stop his daily walk down to nearby Red Deeps. Here he would sit on a bench near the canal, listening to, if not seeing properly, the world go by.

Every day, he would ask mother for a few pennies or sweets to put in his pocket. These he'd give to the tramps that regularly stopped to talk to him as they passed by, before making their way onward to the Nuneaton workhouse, looking for a bed for the night. Father would ask them where they'd travelled from, and what they'd been doing that day, listening to the many tales about life on the road with great interest. Then the tramps would proceed on their way, a sweet or a penny better off.

My mother always worried about him talking to the tramps.

'One day, our Frank,' she'd chide him, 'them tramps er gonna knock you on the 'ead and steal that watch of yours, you mark my words.'

But his reply to this was always the same: 'They won't do me any harm, gel, they're me friends.'

'Well, if they're that good a friend to yer,' she went on, 'why don't you tell 'em to stop chalkin' all over our gate posts? They look a right damn mess.'

Father did talk to one of the regular tramps about it the next day, and was told that the chalk marks were symbols used by the travellers to communicate with each other; that the ones on dad's gateposts were telling other tramps not to make a nuisance of themselves by begging at this house.

The tramps may have had a code of honour, but, sadly, the thief who broke into dad's grandson's home just a few years ago and stole the inscribed gold watch, now a precious family heirloom, obviously had no such scruples. The watch had been left to Jack's son Frankie, on the death of his father. Up until this present time, the watch has never been recovered. It has probably ended up in a private collection of mining artefacts somewhere.

With Frank, Mabel, Jack and Marion now married, this left Ethel, Norman, Mona, Des and myself still at home. I myself never thought Norman would ever get married.

He didn't seem interested in girls; only in sport, his mates, and his home comforts. A favourite brother of mine, I always thought he was the handsomest of the boys. Not quite so stockily built as the others, he was a more lean, athletic type. I suppose I favoured him because he had lots of time for me as a child, taking me for long walks around the countryside, and often buying me sweets, and generally looking after my welfare. So, therefore, I tended to look on him as a kind of protector.

Norman played cricket and darts for Bermuda club, enjoyed gardening, and going out with his mates. Like Jack, he worked at the Measham mine, where he was a timekeeper. Eventually, though, nature took its course, and he met and married a Nuneaton girl named Madge; they had two children, Clive and Wendy.

Sister Ethel was a quiet girl compared with the rest of us. Slim and attractive in her own way, she always wore her hair short and straight; she would never curl it. Musically talented, she could play both the piano and the violin. Content with just a few close friends and her family, she gave up her job as a milliner to stay at home looking after the younger children, when Marion and Mabel left home to get married. It was a shame really, as she was talented at her job, making really beautiful hats.

Ethel still lived at home with us well into marriageable age. Just like Norman, she also was in no hurry to leave the stability of her family life. We all thought she'd end up a spinster, as she didn't seem to bother much with men friends. We were all taken completely by surprise when she announced one day that she was seeing a man: a widower who was quite a few years older than herself.

They had met after she called in for fish and chips at his shop in Coton, Nuneaton. Clarence Wilson's first wife had died in childbirth, and, unable to look after his son himself, he had placed him into the loving care of his sister. So it must have been very distressing for him and Ethel, when, after they married, their first baby was stillborn. Ethel unfortunately was unable to have any more children after this tragedy, but they both knew it wasn't an option to remove Click's son from his sister's home and the caring environment the lad had grown up in. He was far too old now to be uprooted like that.

So they eventually adopted a baby girl they named Moira, and all went to live in Clacton-oSea. Whenen Ethel eventually died, she kindly left a lot of her money to the retired donkey sanctuary there.

Mercia (right) with sister Mona.

MONA

Mona, being the nearest in age to myself, was one of the closest to me of all my siblings. Throughout both our childhood and adulthood, she was never very far away. A pleasant, round faced, strongly built girl, with lovely rosy cheeks, Mona was the picture of health; very different from mine and Mabel's more delicate paler look. Always a bit of a tomboy, and very sporty, Mona was brimming with confidence and vitality. She was never happy unless she had some sort of project on the go to get her teeth into. Life was never going to pass her by in a hurry.

My father called her 'Miss Bossy Boots', because she organised everyone, even if they didn't want her to; her vocation being to save the people in her life from a dull and boring existence.

Mona was the cleverest of us all educationally; and was the only one of us to attend grammar school, where she excelled at most things, especially sport. She represented her school playing hockey, being a brilliant centre forward, and later playing for the textile manufacturers Courtaulds, as this was her place of work. She was also asked to play for the Warwickshire county team, as she was so good. This she refused as she had better things on her mind: her new boyfriend, Albert Ward.

As a child and young adult, Mona had lots of friends, her forthright, sociable personality attracting all types. Like a young Boadicea, Mona gladly took them under her wing, ever ready for a new challenge. Her motto was 'nothing is impossible if you work hard enough at it'; although this could be quite exasperating at times for the person she was trying to reform. She would have been equally at home on a rostrum in Speakers' Corner, Hyde Park.

One of the only times I ever saw Mona really down in the dumps was after she started courting Albert. One night, after being out courting with him and on returning back home, she didn't come in to the parlour to greet us all like she usually did, full of enthusiastic chatter. This was very out of character, as she was always so eager to tell us all what she'd been up to. This time, however, she went straight into the back kitchen instead. Seeking her out, I found her slumped in a chair, with her head resting on the table, and I could see that she'd been crying.

'What's up with you then, Mona,' I asked of her sympathetically. 'Do you want to talk to me about it? Are you not feeling very sociable tonight, or have you had a row with Albert?'

Mona drooped her head further on to her chest, tears still running down her cheeks.

'Daren't let dad see me like this or I'm in big trouble. I've just had the worst experience of my life tonight,' she sobbed.

She went on to tell me all that had happened that evening. How she had met up with Albert as planned, and had gone for a ride on the back of his motorbike, knowing she was doing wrong, as this was strictly forbidden by father. He thought motorbikes unsafe, even though Jack had had one at one time. Mona went on to explain how they'd been travelling slowly up a Nuneaton road in the dark, when suddenly there was a hard impact on the side of Albert's front wheel. This had caused both of them to fall off the bike.

Tragically, it turned out the impact was caused by a little toddler. She had somehow managed to leave her bed under the very noses of her parents, who were listening to the radio in the parlour below. She had crept downstairs into the hallway, and escaped undetected through an unlocked exterior door of her home.

Dressed only in a little vest, she had run straight out into the road and into Albert's wheel, being killed instantly. Mona and Albert were beside themselves, neither of them being able to sleep or eat properly for weeks.

At the inquest, both were found not guilty of any blame, a testifying witness confirming that Albert was riding the bike slowly. A verdict of accidental death was later announced by the court.

Father didn't chastise Mona for being on the motorbike; he thought that she'd suffered enough already.

Though Mona and I were very close, and did most things together, there was sometimes a little bit of the usual jealousy between us. This was never enough to spoil the relationship we had, but caused the usual occasional ripple.

On my part, although I loved her dearly, being younger, I envied Mona her confidence, her ability to take centre stage wherever she went. On Mona's part, she resented the way Father always doted on me, probably because I was the baby of the family.

Just before I left school, Dad asked me not to get a job.

'Stay here at home, Mercia,' he said, 'and look after yer mam and me. You can even come on holiday with us an' all, if you want to.'

Mona, who now worked in the offices at Courtaulds textiles, was listening in to this conversation; and she was livid.

'Why should she go on holiday with yer? We never did. Why can't she get a proper job like the rest of us?' she protested judgementally.

Father soon made it clear to her in no uncertain terms.

'She's stayin' at 'ome cos this is what we both want. Yer mother and miself are not getting any younger, and we want Mercia to look after us, so enough said.'

Three days after I finally left school, Mona came home with an announcement.

'I've got Mercia a job at the factory. A proper job,' she emphasised, 'and she starts tomorrow.'

Dad was so angry with her; but I soon intervened in the argument.

'I'm not having her saying I'm afraid of work, Dad,' I said bitterly. 'I can do a proper job as well as she can, so I'll take it. I'll show her what work is, and I don't mean sittin' on me backside all day like she does either.'

Although disappointed, as he'd been looking forward to my staying at home with them, Father gave in to me eventually; although he wasn't too pleased with Mona for a while, and neither was I.

Despite these normal little family niggles, Mona and I all our lives remained close to each other. Unbeknown to me at the time, though, Mona's intervention in my life on that occasion was, before long, to shape my destiny.

A DEATH IN THE FAMILY

We the siblings were saying goodbye to childhood when father's health started to deteriorate badly. His periods of lethargy prompted mother to get in the doctor, despite his usual objections. Tests were done, and the doctor diagnosed him as having a little-understood malady called diabetes. If it got worse, he was told, he would have to be injected every day with a substance called insulin, and the doctor warned him that his eyes could deteriorate much worse than they already were.

'Well then, doctor,' he answered him dejectedly, 'I'll tell yer this now. It may come to it that I might 'ave to be injected. But I'm no way goin' blind. I'd rather be dead.'

His eyes did get worse quite quickly over the next couple of years. He had to go to the Birmingham eye hospital for treatment regularly. I went with him once to the hospital, and it was the first time I saw my father really cry. He was already having daily injections, but wasn't coping at all with his failing health and eyesight. He sent for the doctor again a few months later, and took him on one side.

'I don't think this treatment is working very well on me, doctor,' he said. 'And I don't want yer takin' any offence by what I'm gonna say next, as there's no offence meant. Cos we've bin friends a long time now, you and me, so we don't need ter pussyfoot around each other, do we? I don't want you comin' 'ere again, doctor, unless it's on a social call. And I ain't takin' any more medicine. I've made up me mind. So thank yer very much for what you've already done fer me. I'm very grateful to yer.'

The doctor was visibly shaken, and absolutely horrified by this statement.

'Do you realise what you are saying to me, Frank Harrison? To withdraw your insulin you'd be giving yourself a death sentence. You can't live without it now.'

'I know what I'm doin',' father replied resolutely. 'Me eyes are really bad now, and as I told yer before, I'm never going blind. I couldn't cope wi' it.

So I'm askin' you kindly this time, don't call again ter see me professionally; only as a friend.'

Despite all our protestations and tears, he remained stubborn: there would be no negotiations, he said. The whole family of us were beside ourselves at his heart-breaking decision. Father must have found it hard not to break down in front of us, seeing the grief his beloved family were displaying. But he was still resolute that he couldn't function as a man without his sight.

Within three months of the doctor's last professional visit, father was dead.

I was newly married at this time and brother Des, who still lived at home, came up to our house to break the bad news. Apparently, father had been lying on the sofa, contentedly listening to the church service on the radio, which he always enjoyed.

Shortly after the programme had finished, he'd said to my mother, 'I'm goin' up to bed now, Emma, cos I feel done in.' So up the stairs he went, cheerfully singing one of the hymns he'd just been listening to. Later that night, mother was woken from her sleep by dad's hands clutching at her shoulder.

'What's the matter, Frank?' she asked, concerned by his actions. 'Are you all right?' When he didn't answer her, she sat up quickly, switched on the bedside lamp and looked down at him.

Sadly, he was already dead. He'd tried to speak to her, but couldn't. There, that night, ended for her a love story that could only end one way.

He was buried in the grounds of his beloved Coton church, where for years he'd been attending the services. Our inconsolable family group, and a multitude of friends, lay this wonderful husband, father and friend to rest, by the side of his eldest son, Thomas. He was only 66 years of age.

Mother lived on for twenty-one years after father died, looked after mainly by my youngest brother Des, who had never married, although he'd had plenty of chances to do so in his youth. With his blond good looks, he had never been short of female admirers; all trying to get a ring on their fingers. Perhaps being the last sibling left at home, he had felt obligated to take care of mother. Or perhaps because he led a very active social life, he thought marriage was too much of a restriction. An affable child and adult, Des enjoyed walking, studying wildlife, and cricket. He had plenty of friends, and they had lots of good times together.

Apart from the episode with Rover and the wasps nest, I can't recall him getting into much trouble at all. When he was about twelve years old, Dad had bought Des a large bell tent, which he erected in the orchard for himself and his pals to camp out in during school holidays. They all had great fun together, sleeping out in all weathers.

When they went off in the daytime, my friends and I would sneak into his camp. We'd sit in his tent, and cook and eat potato skins, beans, and other scraps of food in rusty old tins over the still-hot camp fire. We would then make sure we'd removed all the evidence of our being there, before Des got back home; not prepared to risk a clipped ear.

When he left school, Des was adamant he wasn't going down the pit like all the other boys had, so he took up an apprenticeship with a local butcher. Eventually, though, he did end up working at the mine. I don't know for what reason he changed his mind.

He was a very sporty person, playing most sorts of sports, but excelling at cricket. Being a talented bowler, he played for both Bermuda village and the Warwickshire second team. He also played darts for Bermuda club too.

Des and Marion, like father, both had diabetes in later life, though Marion was much younger than Des when she was diagnosed with it, and died in her early sixties. Des had it at a later age and sadly both his legs were affected and went gangrenous. He never recovered after the first amputation, and died in the hospital.

ANOTHER CHAPTER CLOSES

Mother was bedridden for a while before she died, aged eighty-seven years. My siblings and myself, all married now except for Des, would take turns to sit with her each day, turning her frail little body from time to time to prevent her getting bed sores. She'd practically survived for the last two years on the only food she had really fancied: bread and cheese.

The result of so many pregnancies had eventually taken its toll on her body. Her womb had prolapsed very badly, and for quite a few years now had been giving her lots of trouble. She had to have a device fitted internally that held painkilling drugs. Externally she wore a type of sling which held the womb inside her. Once, while I was changing her bed clothes, I was appalled to see her red, raw-looking womb, lying externally on her thigh. The supportive sling must have come off in the night. She must have suffered so badly with this problem over the years.

Even when she was permanently bedridden and quite weak, Jack the joker could make her laugh. Whenever he came to see her she was in stitches. One day, standing by her bed, he took off all his top clothes, and, clad only in his underpants, pulled back her bed covers.

'Move over now, our Emma' he said, gently pushing her side. 'I'm comin' in wi' yer fer a nap.'

Where she found the energy from I do not know, but she raised herself up indignantly, snatching at the bedclothes.

'No, you blinkin' well are not comin' in 'ere,' she rebuked him loudly. 'You aint getting in here with me wi' no clouts on.'

Pushing him away, her tummy was shaking with mirth under the bed covers. As always, Jack was a tonic for everyone.

Right to the very end of her life, mother remained jovial.Sadly, she deteriorated fast at the end, and hardly spoke; though she knew you were sitting there beside her, and was comforted by it. She started hallucinating, seeing things that weren't really there, such as donkeys and ponies in the field below. But she never complained to us about anything to do with her illness.

After sitting with her most of one day, I was relieved from my post by sister Ethel.

'You get going now, Mercia,' she insisted to me. 'Time to feed that family of yours. You've had a long enough day here already. But first of all tell me how our patient's doing. Any new developments here today?'

I soon filled her in on all the day's events:

'Well, she hasn't eaten anything at all, and she's very quiet. She doesn't seem to be in any pain though, not noticeably anyway. But you're right: The kids will be starving, so I'd better get off now. It's a long old bike ride, the eight miles back home to Bulkington.'

Tired and weary, I arrived back at my home. Mrs Bates, my neighbour, caught up with me just as I was getting off my bike at the gate.

'Sorry, Mercia, to give you some bad news. But I've just had a phone call from your sister Ethel. Your mother's passed away.'

I was mortified, and have always regretted leaving her, and not being with her when she died. Just being there with her, holding her hand, stroking the thin wispy hair from her face, easing her passage from one world to the other together. But it was not to be.

When she was alive, and I was just a child, I always used to tell her that I never wanted to see her dead; that I only wanted to remember her as she was in life. I often wonder if she purposely clung on that extra hour longer, until I had left the house that day.

In Father's will, he had stated that after mother died everything in the house had to be sold, right down to the last teaspoon. The money from the sale was then to be divided between we siblings. Eldest brother Frank was the executor of the will, but for some reason didn't carry out father's wishes, letting members of the family take what they wanted from the house, on a first-come first-served basis. I didn't go back for a while, it being too painful an experience for me at the time.

I couldn't face going into the family home, knowing that mother wasn't in it any more. So the only memento I had from the house to remember her by was her wedding ring, which was given to me later. I've treasured this symbol of her union with my father always.

I never had the chance to say goodbye after she died.

In our family it was a tradition that only the men of the family attended the funerals. Mother was buried in Coton church, Nuneaton, alongside my father and her first-born son, Thomas.

Mercia aged 18 years.

THE END OF AN ERA

Mona had now married her gentle Albert. And later I had married my dark-haired man who I'd met at a party. He was the brother of a friend who worked with me at the Courtaulds fabrics factory.

Mona's intervention into my life a few years earlier, when she'd got me the job there, had indirectly turned out to be the best thing that ever happened to me.

The friend in question was a girl called Poppy Oliver, and we worked together on the same job. Poppy was a good friend; a very pleasant, chatty girl, but was a little prim, even a bit prudish – which was not surprising, after being brought up by a very strict mother. She still wore clothes that showed little or no flesh, which wasn't the present fashion at all, hem lengths now being much shorter and necklines lower.

Poppy had started dating a nice young man named Harry Owen, who, I suspect, wouldn't have got within an arm's length of Poppy if his intentions hadn't been 110% honourable. I myself wasn't seeing anybody seriously at this time, so I was quite pleased when one day Poppy asked me:

'Mercia, how do you fancy goin' out on a blind date? We're having a party at home this weekend, and Harry's brother is coming with him. I know he fancies you, and it'll make up a nice foursome.'

I'd met Chris Owen, Harry's brother, once before, and had found him to be a pleasant, sociable chap, and not bad looking either.

'Maybe I might take you up on that offer, Poppy,' I replied cheerfully. 'I've nothing special on this weekend, and you never know, love could blossom. We could even become sisters-in-law as well as best friends.' Poppy giggled quietly to herself at the thought of it all.

When the night of the party finally arrived, I dressed myself up to the nines, wanting to impress my date; and was quite pleased with the overall result that reflected in my bedroom mirror.

Going downstairs, I went into the drawing room to await my lift to Coventry. Mona and Dad were in there too, both reading the daily newspapers.

'You look nice, doesn't she, Dad?' commented Mona, dropping the paper on the table, before turning me round to fasten one of the small buttons I'd missed on the back of my dress.

'She does,' he replied rather wistfully, as if suddenly realising his youngest child was now a grown-up woman, and not his little girl any more.

This expression only remained on his face for a minute though, before it broke into a huge grin.

'You want to know something, our Mercia?' he chuckled merrily. 'You're gettin' a chest on you, just like a young cuckoo!'

When I eventually arrived at the party, it was in full swing, and I was greeted by a very excited Poppy.

'Come into the kitchen and I'll take your coat,' she said, grinning like a Cheshire cat.

She pushed me ahead of her into the tiny little room, before pulling off my coat. Suddenly, the smile left her face, and was replaced by a deep flush of scarlet, as she gazed awkwardly at my dress, clearly embarrassed by it.

Clutching at the brooch that held together the neat little lace collar at the base of her throat, Poppy spoke in a low, whispering voice.

'Mercia, I don't quite know how to put this to you. Your dress, it's really lovely, but it is a bit revealing. You're actually showing the top bit of your cleavage.

Would you like to borrow one of my little lace hankies, to pop into the top of it?'

Giving her a huge hug, I laughed loudly at her primness.'No thanks, Poppy. I think I'll give the hanky a miss tonight, because I'm wearin' this dress for a reason; the reason being that you asked me here tonight to catch myself a man. So I'm settin' the trap.'

The smile soon appeared back on Poppy's face on my last comment, and the previous conversation was soon forgotten after we joined the party.

Chris Owen was the perfect gentleman, and I found him very good company. I was also introduced to some of the friends and family of Poppy, who I hadn't met before. All in all, it was a great party, and I was thoroughly enjoying myself.

Some hours later, the party was in full swing, the consumed alcohol bringing even the more reserved people into the middle of the floor to dance. Eventually, my sore feet indicated to me that I should sit down and give them a rest, which I did reluctantly. Sitting back down in my chair, I soon became deeply engrossed in conversation with Chris; and, as we chatted on and on amiably, I just happened to glance across the room as we talked, and found my eyes locked into those of a complete stranger, who was standing at the back of the room watching me.

Tearing my gaze away from his, I tried to pretend that he wasn't there, but found myself periodically looking at him again and again, and often found his dark brown, almost black eyes boring into mine. I whispered to Poppy when I had the chance.

'Who's that man, the one standing at the back of the room by the door?'

'Which man?' she asked of me curiously, her eyes following in the direction of mine.

'The tall, slim, dark haired one with the tanned face, wearing the uniform,' I gestured discretely.

'Oh, him, she giggled amiably, 'that's my older brother Jim; he's home on leave. He spends most of the time abroad with his regiment. He's based in Egypt at the moment.'

Intrigued, I turned back to Chris and we continued our conversation. We were still chatting away to each other, putting the world to rights, when, suddenly, the light from the room was almost obliterated by the shadow of a man now standing over us.

'Would it be appropriate for me to have this next dance please, with your lady?' a clear, rather refined voice asked of Chris, who, stunned for words, nodded reluctantly.

'May I,' he then enquired of me, offering his arm before whisking me on to the dance floor, joining the throng of happy partygoers having an equally good time.

Circling my waist with his arms, my body felt on fire. I could feel his lips brushing against my hair. The electricity between us was really sparking, and I felt breathless and light headed as he held me close to him. Suddenly, the psychic prediction given to me by Sarah Poutney flooded through my mind.

'I see sand, pyramids, and camels. I also see a tall, dark-skinned man. Once you meet him, nothing will part you, only death.'

And it was only Jim's death that did part us.

Poppy was a bit miffed with me for a while, which was quite understandable. I too felt really guilty about Chris Owen, whom I liked very much. But our destinies are mapped out for us before we are even born; and there's nothing we can do to change them.

Jim had to return to Egypt, but the mould was now set and we later married.

'What was it that attracted you to me the most?' I asked of him one day, just out of curiosity.

'I'm sure it had to be that magnificent bosom,' he replied, with a twinkle in his eye. Always the romantic!

He loved the song 'Some Enchanted Evening' from the musical *South Pacific*. It was always one of his favourites; its words, he said, echoed that night we met across that crowded room.

Just before I got married, I decided to give up my job at the Courtaulds factory.

Father had recently bought a shop with living accommodation behind it, in nearby Coton. He had told myself and Jim that we could live there behind the shop after we were married, as this would give us a chance to save up for a place of our own later. I asked Father what he was intending to do with the shop, but he wasn't sure yet.

'How about me taking on the shop then?' I enquired of him one day. 'I really fancy doin' something different with my life. Jim and I will be getting married as soon as he finishes in the army next month, and obviously we'll be livin' behind the shop. So how about we rent it off you, instead of someone else? I could turn it into a hairdressers. I've always fancied doing that job.'

Father agreed to let me have a go at the hairdressing. He asked Connie Swain, a highly recommended local hairdresser, if she would be interested in training me up; also if she'd be interested in working in the shop too. Connie agreed to what father had proposed. A very accomplished hairdresser herself, she quickly and thoroughly showed me how to cut, perm, colour, and style hair.

The salon was fitted out with sinks and hairdryers, and a huge newfangled perming machine was suspended from the ceiling. This fearsome-looking monstrosity resembled an oversized milking machine, with its many cupped tentacles hanging down from it. Pulled down from the ceiling when in use, the cups were placed over the client's hair, which had already been primed with a perming solution.

The result, after a quick heating up by the machine, was an abundance of tight curls.

Jim and I were married at last, and we moved into our new home behind the shop. Mona, who was already married to Albert, lived nearby, so we enjoyed a good social life together as a foursome. The shop was doing well and I was enjoying the work. Life at this time was happy and problem-free.

But this karma was not to last. My hands started itching a lot after handling the hairdressing solutions, eventually breaking out into sores between my fingers. I couldn't wear rubber gloves because in those days they were too bulky, preventing me from putting curlers in properly. I went to see the doctor, who diagnosed industrial dermatitis. He gave me numerous ointments and barrier creams, which helped but didn't solve the problem.

Within six months, the insides of my hands were just skinless, raw flesh. Every night before going to bed I would cover them with ointment before donning a pair of cotton gloves. The next morning there would be a new skin forming over them, but as soon as I stretched out my fingers, this would break. Worse was yet to come. Suddenly, my hair started to fall out too, leaving bald patches. I had to wear a turban all the time, with just a kiss curl of hair peeping out over my forehead. This headgear I wore for months, which did nothing at all for my ego.

The doctor said it would never get better until I got away from the chemicals; my dream job, it seems, was now over.

The shop was eventually put up for sale; Connie, who was nearing retirement age, keeping it going until it was sold. The new owners wanted the flat too, so Jim and I moved away to the little village of Bulkington, eight miles away from Nuneaton, but still in Warwickshire. Mona and Albert later surprised us by moving into a house nearly opposite to us. My hands, thank goodness, were now fully healed, and my hair had grown back to its normal thickness.

We all led a happy existence there for the next few years, enjoying life as young couples do; having a good social life, and not too many worries.

Jim, after finishing his army career, had got a decent enough job; which was lucky, as World War II was just beginning in England at this stage. World War II was to have its consequences for us all, though, because, as it raged on, supplies of most things got short. Subsequently, the government had to look elsewhere for the war effort's needs.

Quinine became one of the things in short supply; this being urgently needed to treat malaria symptoms in soldiers serving abroad. The result to Mona and myself, and many other women, was unplanned babies. The pessaries we used for birth control, which contained quinine, suddenly weren't working as efficiently as they used to.

Mona, already having two sons, Terry and Adrian, soon found herself pregnant again with another son, Trevor. He was quickly followed by twins, Cedric and a long-awaited daughter, Angela.

I myself, who only wanted and had got one child – a daughter, Nina – found myself pregnant again with my son, Peter, followed by another daughter, Geraldine. Our lives became very busy: no time for relaxation in the daytime, only when the children were in bed at night, and all the chores were finally finished.

If Mona wanted to go shopping or somewhere else, I'd have all the children, and, vice versa, she'd have mine. If one of us was taken ill, then the other one would take over the children until our husbands came home from work. At times my veranda could be holding up to six prams as young children, toddlers, and babies enjoyed their afternoon naps.

Mona and I remained very close until the day she died, which happened to be on my birthday. I missed her strong personality, and her great sense of humour, and can still visualise her laughing, her rotund little tummy shaking up and down with mirth. She was still 'Miss Bossy Boots', as father used to call her: organising committees, social outings, church events and women's institutes well into her eighties. What a woman she was, until cancer reared its ugly head and took her from us. I miss her and the rest of my family greatly.

Now, though, it all seems such a long time ago. My own children are married and have grown-up children of their own; grown-up grandchildren too. I myself am now in my ninety-seventh year; the only one remaining of my original birth family.

The old house in Bermuda, 'The Pumps', has been long gone, making way for an industrial estate. The house on Hilltop is still there though, and hasn't changed at all.

Also long gone is my beloved husband, James Stephen Oliver. We were, indeed, a match made in heaven.

My daughter's researching for this book has brought back many memories, some bad, but most of them good.

I still grieve deep down inside myself for the loss of the family who enriched my life so much.

And one day in the future will look forward to meeting them all again.

Thanks to this book, my memories will not die with me. They have shown that life was not all bad, for those living In The Shadow Of The Wheel.

Mercia today, aged 97 years.

EPILOGUE

The face of mining has changed drastically during my lifetime, as everything gradually became mechanised. The horses and ponies used in mining have long since died, after being retired to the lush grassy fields of the animal sanctuaries, to finish off their hard-working lives in quiet rest.

These were later replaced by huge lorries and underground motorised rail systems. No more back-breaking pushing and pulling of coal tubs, by man or beast. The miners pick no longer strikes the stubborn black surfaces of the face, trying to persuade it to give up its booty; the man in question half-stripped, shiny with the sweat of his exertions.

Instead, huge motorised circular cutters, edged with teeth as hard as diamonds, now do the job, cutting through the coal face like a knife through butter, and bringing down more coal in a day than a shift of men in my father's time could have cut out in a month.

Mine safety became paramount too: new technology bringing mine accidents to a minimum. Rarely now would the heart-stopping sound of the emergency hooters be heard any more; its eerie wailing piercing the hearts of all who heard it.

No more working waist high in water, as my ancestors did, dragging their weary bodies home on the brink of exhaustion. Those days, thank goodness, are now long gone. Lungs around the world did and still do get blackened by coal dust, leaving behind a legacy of crippled men, whose families are still fighting for compensation to this day.

But progress, as always, has had its ups and its downs.

On the plus side, as wages became better, the miners were able to buy or rent their own houses; no fear of an eviction any more. Workhouses, too, became a thing of the past. Though, on reflection, dismal and terrifying as they were in the earlier days, later they played an important role.

Many of today's families owe their existence to these cold, impersonal institutions, which gave their ancestors the chance of living, even if it was at a price.

Then, just as the face of mining seemed to be at its best for all concerned, everything had changed again for the miners of England and Wales. Just as the country became more affluent, people also became more materialistic.

Though the coal was still being used in industry, as families became richer and 'posher', the housewife decided she didn't want the dust and dirt of an open coal fire any more.

Installing those new-fangled oil fires, then radiators, had such a devastating effect on the coal industry. The government put the final nail in the coffin by importing coal from other countries, such as Poland and other places, claiming it was cheaper to do this than to extract it from our own mines.

One by one, most of the pits have now closed down; very few are still operating compared with years ago. Men who had descended from generations of miners, as my father and brothers had, were finding themselves no longer standing at the pit gates waiting to start work. But, instead, they were standing in the dole queue, looking for jobs that didn't exist. Everything for them over the years had now turned full circle.

There are still many people out there, mostly the older generation, who still prefer the wonderful sight and feel of a roaring coal fire, cheerful and glowing in the fire grate on a cold winter's night, bringing relaxation and a flush to the cheeks that could never be achieved by any radiator.

I myself believe the mines will open up again in time, though not in my lifetime, obviously. As fuels such as oil and natural gas deplete with time, fossil fuel could once again be needed to keep the world going.

What a lovely thought that, once again, we might hear the wonderful sound of the miners' male voice choirs, their melodious voices raised in song, echoing around the fields and valleys of England and Wales, just like they did in the old days.